THE GIFT OF GENDER

THE GIFT OF GENDER

8 sessions on the roles of men and women

by Judy and Jack Balswick
Allen and Margery Corben

Scripture quotations are taken from the *Holy Bible, New International Version,* © 1973, 1978, 1984, International Bible Society. Used by permission of Zondervan Bible Publishers.

Recommended Dewey Decimal Classification: 301.402
Suggested Subject Heading: SMALL GROUPS

Library of Congress Catalog Card Number: 91-65454
ISBN: 0-89693-882-4

1 2 3 4 5 6 7 8 9 10 Printing / Year 95 94 93 92 91

VICTOR BOOKS
A division of SP Publications, Inc.
Wheaton, Illinois 60187

CONTENTS

PURPOSE: To gain an understanding of what it means to be a woman and a man today.

INTRODUCTION

The Gift of Gender is for people who want to gain a Christian understanding of what it means to be a woman and a man today. An in-depth Leader's Guide is included at the back of the book with suggested time guidelines to help you structure your emphases. Each of the 8 sessions contains the following elements:

❑ **GroupSpeak**—quotes from group members that capsulize what the session is about.

❑ **Getting Acquainted**—activities or selected readings to help you begin thinking and sharing from your life and experiences about the subject of the session. Use only those options that seem appropriate for your group.

❑ **Gaining Insight**—questions and in-depth Bible study help you gain principles from Scripture for life-related application.

❑ **Growing By Doing**—an opportunity to practice the Truth learned in the Gaining Insight section.

❑ **Going The Second Mile**—a personal enrichment section for you to do on your own.

❑ **Growing As A Leader**—an additional section in the Leader's Guide for the development and assessment of leadership skills.

❑ **Pocket Principles**—brief guidelines inserted in the Leader's Guide to help the Group Leader learn small group leadership skills as needed.

❑ **Session Objectives**—goals listed in the Leader's Guide that describe what should happen in the group by the end of the session.

IS THIS YOUR FIRST SMALL GROUP?

’smol grüp: A limited number of individuals assembled together having some unifying relationship.

Kris’chən ’smol grüp: 4–12 persons who meet together on a regular basis, over a determined period of time, for the shared purpose of pursuing biblical truth. They seek to mature in Christ and become equipped to serve as His ministers in the world.

Picture Your First Small Group.

List some words that describe what you want your small group to look like.

What Kind Of Small Group Do You Have?

People form all kinds of groups based on gender, age, marital status, and so forth. There are advantages and disadvantages to each. Here are just a few:

❑ **Same Age Groups** will probably share similar needs and interests.

- ❑ **Intergenerational Groups** bring together people with different perspectives and life experiences.

- ❑ **Men's or Women's Groups** usually allow greater freedom in sharing and deal with more focused topics.

- ❑ **Singles or Married Groups** determine their relationship emphases based on the needs of a particular marital status.

- ❑ **Mixed Gender Groups (singles and/or couples)** stimulate interaction and broaden viewpoints while reflecting varied lifestyles.

However, the most important area of "alikeness" to consider when forming a group is an **agreed-on purpose.** Differences in purpose will sabotage your group and keep its members from bonding. If, for example, Mark wants to pray but not play while Jan's goal is to learn through playing, then Mark and Jan's group will probably not go anywhere. People need different groups at different times in their lives. Some groups will focus on sharing and accountability, some on work projects or service, and others on worship. *Your small group must be made up of persons who have similar goals.*

How Big Should Your Small Group Be?

The **fewest** people to include would be **4.** Accountability will be high, but absenteeism may become a problem.

The **most** to include would be **12.** But you will need to subdivide regularly into groups of 3 or 4 if you want people to feel cared for and to have time for sharing.

How Long Should You Meet?

8 Weeks gives you a start toward becoming a close community, but doesn't overburden busy schedules. Count on needing three or four weeks to develop a significant trust level. The smaller the group, the more quickly trust develops.

Weekly Meetings will establish bonding at a good pace and allow for accountability. The least you can meet and still be an effective group is once a month. If you choose the latter, work at individual contact among group members between meetings.

You will need **75 minutes** to accomplish a quality meeting. The larger the size, the more time it takes to become a healthy group. Serving refreshments will add 20–30 minutes, and singing and/or prayer time, another 20–30 minutes. Your time duration may be determined by the time of day you meet and by the amount of energy members bring to the group. Better to start small and ask for more time when it is needed because of growth.

What Will Your Group Do?

To be effective, each small group meeting should include:

1. **Sharing**—You need to share who you are and what is happening in your life. This serves as a basis for relationship building and becomes a springboard for searching out scriptural truth.

2. **Scripture**—There must always be biblical input from the Lord to teach, rebuke, correct, and train in right living. Such material serves to move your group in the direction of maturity in Christ and protects from pooled ignorance and distorted introspection.

3. **Truth in practice**—It is vital to provide opportunities for *doing* the Word of God. Experiencing this within the group insures greater likelihood that insights gained will be utilized in everyday living.

Other elements your group may wish to add to these three are: a time of **worship, specific prayer** for group members, **shared projects**, a time to **socialize** and enjoy **refreshments**, and **recreation.**

ONE

A Traditional Look at Women and Men

GroupSpeak: *"I knew what I thought about women and men, but I didn't know why. We explored scriptural, family, and cultural bases for what we think. It was really surprising to discover that a lot of my assumptions were not the same as other people's in the group. I expect we'll have a lot of good discussions in the weeks to come."*

A Balanced Picture

Do we live, with Garrison Keillor, in a Lake Woebegon world where we see all the women as strong, all the men as good-looking, and all our children as above average? Or do we have a more balanced picture of people as individuals, each with their own characteristics?

Just where *do* we base the decisions which shape our mental images of what it means to be a woman or a man? This session will introduce the ideas of manhood and womanhood, and help us explore our sources for female and male images.

GETTING ACQUAINTED

Good Folk

Write down some characteristics that you think are good qualities for people to have. One way to do this is to think of a few good folk that you know, and list some of their qualities. Or you could think of three famous people whom you admire. In any case, this list is for you alone. No one else will be looking at it, unless *you* choose to show it to them, so feel free to write whatever you wish.

Kin Folk

We often get some of our life definitions from other members of our families. Did you include any of your relatives above? Can you think of why or why not? Write some reasons below.

Have you ever looked at your family's genealogy? A simple genealogy can be a useful way to come to grips with *why* we believe *what* we believe about gender (and other!) issues.

Here is a way to do a genogram (a simple genealogy diagram) which can be used in a variety of ways to look at family. Starting near the bottom of the space provided, draw a square for yourself if you are a man, or a circle if you are a woman. Draw a line up to intersect with the line between your parents, and draw their lines up to your grandparents. Now draw in any siblings and/or spouse next to yourself, and lines down to any children. Write names in the circles and squares. Go farther and include people in any generation who were or are important women or men for you. Use a pencil and be prepared to erase to give yourself room. Here is a model:

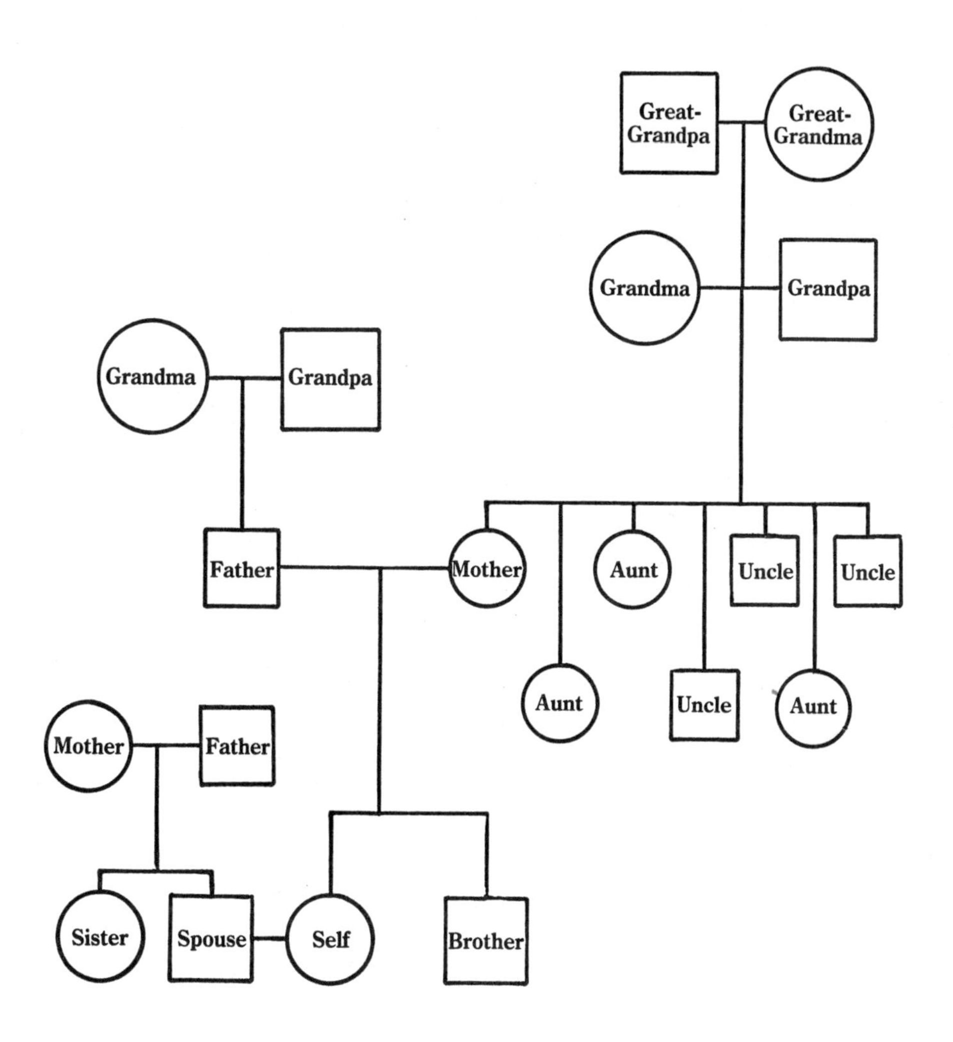

MY GENOGRAM

From your genogram, consider the following questions:

How far back can you *name* people on each side of your family tree?

How many of these people did/do you actually know?

What do you know about your ancestors?

Did anyone ever do something really at odds with social propriety? What was it?

What is the most important memory you have of a female figure in your genogram?

A male figure?

On your genogram, write in the positive qualities that you see these people as having. Don't forget yourself! You might include near the genogram any people that you consider to be part of your spiritual family: perhaps a wise teacher who helped make sure you were headed in the right direction, or a friend you worked with once upon a time who told you stories that made you want to do something special with your life.

GAINING INSIGHT

Scripture Study
Read the following passages.

[26]Then God said, "Let Us make humankind in Our image, in Our likeness; and let them rule over the fish of the sea and

the birds of the air, over the livestock, over all the earth, and over all the creatures that move along the ground." [27]So God created man in His own image, in the image of God He created him; male and female He created them.

Genesis 1:26-27

[22]But [in contrast to the works of the flesh], the fruit of the Spirit is love, joy, peace, patience, kindness, goodness, faithfulness, [23]gentleness and self-control. Against such things there is no law.

Galatians 5:22-23

What do you see in these passages about positive character qualities of women?

Positive traits in men?

What new idea(s) do you have about Christian character and gender after having read these passages?

Or what idea(s) have you found reinforced by these passages?

What does Scripture say is true about human beings?

About women and men?

As you see it, are these different or the same? Why?

GROWING BY DOING

Sharing
With another person in the group, share a time when you were younger that a person of either gender impressed you with their positive character. How did that person demonstrate or model that positive trait for you?

How are you like (or in what ways do you wish to be like) that person?

How could you begin this week to become a model for someone younger than you in this area?

GOING THE SECOND MILE

Media Exploration
Before the next time we meet, spend some time exploring the media for images of positive character qualities. Also look for distortions of male and female in our culture. How are the people in these images relating to each other? What would happen in the next few minutes to the people in these ads? Complete their story in a sentence or two. Collect pictures from magazines, or jot down images that you notice here.

TWO

Liberated Men and Women

GroupSpeak: *"I had always thought of being 'liberated' as being liberated from sin, but this session talked about being liberated from ideas. I hadn't realized how difficult it would be to break free from some of the notions of what a man or a woman is. And I had never noticed how much I didn't like the images for myself on television, even when I was laughing about them!"*

Liberated From What?
What does it mean to be liberated? The dictionary says "to be set free from restraint or bondage." What are liberated men liberated from? What are liberated women liberated from? What does "liberated" mean for people in the church? Are Christians liberated *from* anything? What? Liberated to do what?

In this session, we will be trying to get some insight into these questions. Spend some time thinking about how Jesus has liberated us in the particular area of gender.

GETTING ACQUAINTED

The Power Line
How powerful you felt (and feel currently) in the different spheres of your life may make it easier or harder to be "liber-

ated" in the area of gender. Doing something socially unexpected requires a certain amount of personal power. Liberation in this context is the ability to overcome the expectations other people have, and that takes power. For example, testifying to your faith in Christ before those who do not believe requires power; so does saying "no" to drugs.

How powerful do you feel in the spheres below? Use the spaces to write in some words and memories which come to mind.

School	________________	Peers	________________
	________________		________________
Family	________________	Work	________________
	________________		________________
Church	________________	Sports	________________
	________________		________________

GAINING INSIGHT

Free From Stereotypes

A part of being truly liberated is to be free from needing to conform to our cultural stereotypes of gender roles. Here are some biblical examples of people doing powerful, meaningful things. Read the passage and write down what is unusual (or atypical) about what they are doing.

[24]Meanwhile a Jew named Apollos, a native of Alexandria, came to Ephesus. He was a learned man, with a thorough knowledge of the Scriptures. [25]He had been instructed in the way of the Lord, and he spoke with great fervor and taught about Jesus accurately, though he knew only the baptism of John. [26]He began to speak boldly in the synagogue. When Priscilla and Aquila heard him, they invited him to their home and explained to him the way of God more adequately.

Acts 18:24-26

Priscilla—

[38]As Jesus and His disciples were on their way, He came to a village where a woman named Martha opened her home to Him. [39]She had a sister called Mary, who sat at the Lord's feet listening to what He said.

Luke 10:38-39

[21]"Lord," Martha said to Jesus, "if You had been here, my brother would not have died. [22]But I know that even now God will give You whatever You ask."

[23]Jesus said to her, "Your brother will rise again."

[24]Martha answered, "I know he will rise again in the resurrection at the last day."

[25]Jesus said to her, "I am the resurrection and the life. He who believes in Me will live, even though he dies; [26]and whoever lives and believes in Me will never die. Do you believe this?"

John 11:21-26

Mary, Lazarus' sister—

[19]While Pilate was sitting on the judge's seat, his wife sent him this message: "Don't have anything to do with that innocent man, for I have suffered a great deal today in a dream because of Him."

Matthew 27:19

Pilate's wife—

[1]After Ehud died, the Israelites once again did evil in the eyes of the LORD. [2]So the LORD sold them into the hands of Jabin, a king of Canaan, who reigned in Hazor. The commander of his army was Sisera, who lived in Harosheth Haggoyim. [3]Because he had nine hundred iron chariots and had cruelly oppressed the Israelites for twenty years, they cried to the LORD for help.

[4]Deborah, a prophetess, the wife of Lappidoth, was leading Israel at that time. [5]She held court under the Palm of Deborah . . . and the Israelites came to her to have their disputes decided.

Judges 4:1-5

Deborah—

[14]Hilkiah the priest, Ahikam, Acbor, Shaphan and Asaiah went to speak to the prophetess Huldah, . . . [15]She said to them, "This is what the LORD, the God of Israel, says: Tell the man who sent you to me, [16]'This is what the LORD says: I am going to bring disaster on this place and its people, according to everything written in the book the king of Judah has read. . . .' "

2 Kings 22:14-16

Huldah—

[1]After this, Jesus traveled about from one town and village to another, proclaiming the good news of the kingdom of God. The Twelve were with Him, [2]and also some women who had been cured of evil spirits and diseases: Mary (called Magdalene) from whom seven demons had come out; [3]Joanna the wife of Cuza, the manager of Herod's household; Susanna; and many others. These women were helping to support them out of their own means.

Luke 8:1-3

Joanna—

[31]"Therefore I wail over Moab, for all Moab I cry out, I moan for the men of Kir Hareseth. [32]I weep for you, as Jazer weeps, O vines of Sibmah. Your branches spread as far as the sea; they reached as far as the sea of Jazer. The destroyer has fallen on your ripened fruit and grapes.

. . . [36]So My heart laments for Moab like a flute; it laments like a flute for the men of Kir Hareseth. The wealth they acquired is gone. . . . [38]On all the roofs in Moab and in the public squares there is nothing but mourning, for I have broken Moab like a jar that no one wants," declares the LORD.

Jeremiah 48:31-32, 36, 38

God—

[35]Jesus wept.

John 11:35

Jesus—

[1]How beautiful you are, my darling! Oh, how beautiful! Your eyes behind your veil are doves. Your hair is like a flock of goats descending from Mount Gilead.

Song of Songs 4:1

Solomon—

[7]But we were gentle among you, like a mother caring for her little children. [8]We loved you so much that we were delighted to share with you not only the Gospel of God but our lives as well, because you had become so dear to us.

1 Thessalonians 2:7-8

Paul—

[20]Peter turned and saw that the disciple whom Jesus loved was following them. (This was the one who had leaned

back against Jesus at the supper and had said, "Lord, who is going to betray You?")

John 21:20

John—

[10]I will weep and wail for the mountains and take up a lament concerning the desert pastures.

Jeremiah 9:10

Jeremiah—

[22]I, Tertius, who wrote down this letter, greet you in the Lord.

Romans 16:22

Tertius—

Now read Mark 10:42-45.

[42]Jesus called them together and said, "You know that those who are regarded as rulers of the Gentiles lord it over them, and their high officials exercise authority over them. [43]Not so with you. Instead, whoever wants to become great among you must be your servant, [44]and whoever wants to be first must be slave of all. [45]For even the Son of Man did not come to be served, but to serve, and to give His life as a ransom for many."

Mark 10:42-45

Jesus is describing a kind of relationship which employs power when He says, "Not so with you." Describe in your own words the relationship Jesus is opposing.

Is what Jesus is opposing a barrier to holiness? How?

The following passage describes the first Christians.

[42]They devoted themselves to the apostles' teaching and to the fellowship, to the breaking of bread and to prayer. [43]Everyone was filled with awe, and many wonders and miraculous signs were done by the apostles. [44]All the believers were together and had everything in common. [45]Selling their possessions and goods, they gave to anyone as he had need. [46]Every day they continued to meet together with glad and sincere hearts, [47]praising God and enjoying the favor of all the people. And the Lord added to their number daily those who were being saved.

Acts 2:42-47

Was the early church successful in following Jesus' command about not being like the Gentiles? Why or why not?

Can you name some contemporary institutions or organizations that follow the pattern of authority Jesus said not to imitate?

Name some that follow another pattern or authority, and how they do so.

GROWING BY DOING

Stereotypes

Spend 10 minutes coming up with contemporary models of powerful and competent behavior. Name and describe a person of the opposite gender doing something well that you would like to be able to do and why. Some examples might include public speaking, cooking, sports, art, sewing, etc. Explain why this action is possible (or impossible) for you to do.

Take a moment to discuss the images you collected this past week from the media. If you collected scenes on TV, explain the scene to the group and what it reveals about how men and women interact. If you collected ads from magazines or the newspaper, note the relationships (physical/spacial) between men and women. Do they idealize the bodies of women or men? Are real people shown, or only airbrushed versions?

There are a number of standard images that advertisers rely on as a kind of shorthand to communicate to people. Think about your collected ads and TV scenes. What are some of these stereotypical images?

How many of these images are positive? How many are negative? Have you ever noticed these before?

GOING THE SECOND MILE

Freedom to Go Outside the Boundaries
Try something atypical for your gender. Here are some suggestions that start out easy and get harder.

For Women
- ❑ Consider going without makeup for a day.
- ❑ Consider making a suggestion to the boss in front of other people.

- ❑ Promise yourself that for one day you will do no one's work but your own (not even your family's), no matter how urgently you are asked.

For Men

- ❑ Consider asking another person if he or she likes what you're wearing. Watch for people's reactions.
- ❑ Consider making coffee for everyone at the office.
- ❑ Promise yourself that you will try to spend one day never interrupting another person or even starting to talk before they have completely finished.

Brainstorm some other possibilities. Report back to the group next week about the reactions you got.

Recall what people said they wanted to do. Choose one person and pray at least once during the coming week that God will help that person accomplish his or her atypical task.

For the next session, think about some of the issues raised about stereotypes and power, and relate that to your friendships, both same and mixed gender.

THREE

Friendship and Gender

GroupSpeak: *"I noticed ways in which my childhood and current friendships follow similar and different patterns. I would like to know how to have friendships with members of the opposite sex, and sometimes it's difficult to sort out the boundaries. It was good to work through how to define boundaries in ways that can strengthen my friendships with members of both genders."*

In His Image

Being created in God's image suggests that we are created to be in relationship with others. The Holy Trinity depicts a relationship between three Persons. Genesis describes creation in relational terms: "Let *Us* make man in *Our* image" (Genesis 1:26). Love, unity, and service are themes in the New Testament for relationships within the body of Christ.

Christ calls us His friends when we do the will of God (John 17). Jesus spent time with His own friends in a variety of settings (wedding feast, private dining, walking, fishing, talking) and longed for His intimate friends to be with Him in His deepest times of trouble. His relationship with John was especially tender. Mary, who anointed His feet, was intimately connected with Him in this act of love. In a modern and impersonal world we also need our special "cuddle/support" group of friends to be intimate with.

Friendship is part of God's design. We are challenged to understand *how* we are to be in relationships with both opposite and same gender friends. Let's take this time to consider our friendships and the impact gender has on these relationships.

GETTING ACQUAINTED

Friends are gifts from God and we cherish these relationships. We establish friendships early in life with brothers, sisters, cousins, and playmates. Have you ever considered the importance of these friends and how they have contributed to your life? The relationships established with our peers in early life influence how we interact with others in our present life.

Early Friendships
Take a moment to think about your early friendships. List the names and some memories of your most important childhood friends:

FRIEND	ACTIVITY/MEMORY

Reflect—Did you have both same and opposite gender friends? Was there a difference in how you related to friends of the same and opposite gender?

My Special Friend
Now, choose a special friend in your current life and focus on why this person is so important to you. Consider a special activity you do together. In a few minutes you will have an

opportunity to share about this friend with another group member.

Did you notice any particular patterns when you compared childhood and current choice of friend and/or activities?

GAINING INSIGHT

Understanding Friendship

Focus on the dynamics in these friendships found in the Bible. Identify the special qualities of these relationships.

[1]After David had finished talking with Saul, Jonathan became one in spirit with David, and he loved him as himself. . . . [3]And Jonathan made a covenant with David because he loved him as himself. [4]Jonathan took off the robe he was wearing and gave it to David, along with his tunic, and even his sword, his bow and his belt.

1 Samuel 18:1, 3-4

David and Jonathan—

[15]"Look," said Naomi, "your sister-in-law is going back to her people and her gods. Go back with her."

[16]But Ruth replied, "Don't urge me to leave you or to turn back from you. Where you go I will go, and where you stay I will stay. Your people will be my people and your God my God. [17]Where you die I will die, and there I will be buried. May the LORD deal with me, be it ever so severely, if anything but death separates you and me."

Ruth 1:15-17

Ruth and Naomi—

[11]When Job's three friends, Eliphaz the Temanite, Bildad the Shuhite and Zophar the Naamathite, heard about all the troubles that had come upon him, they set out from their homes and met together by agreement to go and sympathize with him and comfort him. [12]When they saw him from a distance, they could hardly recognize him; they began to weep aloud, and they tore their robes and sprinkled dust on their heads. [13]Then they sat on the ground with him for seven days and seven nights. No one said a word to him, because they saw how great his suffering was.

Job and his friends—

[39]At that time Mary got ready and hurried to a town in the hill country of Judea, [40]where she entered Zechariah's home and greeted Elizabeth. [41]When Elizabeth heard Mary's greeting, the baby leaped in her womb, and Elizabeth was filled with the Holy Spirit. [42]In a loud voice she exclaimed: "Blessed are you among women, and blessed is the child you will bear! [43]But why am I so favored, that the mother of my Lord should come to me? [44]As soon as the sound of your greeting reached my ears, the baby in my womb leaped for joy. [45]Blessed is she who has believed that what the Lord has said to her will be accomplished!" . . . [56]Mary stayed with Elizabeth for about three months and then returned home.

Luke 1:39-45, 56

Mary and Elizabeth—

[22]News of this reached the ears of the church at Jerusalem, and they sent Barnabas to Antioch. [23]When he arrived and saw the evidence of the grace of God, he was glad

and encouraged them all to remain true to the Lord with all their hearts. [24]He was a good man, full of the Holy Spirit and faith, and a great number of people were brought to the Lord.

[25]Then Barnabas went to Tarsus to look for Saul, [26]and when he found him, he brought him to Antioch. So for a whole year Barnabas and Saul met with the church and taught great numbers of people. The disciples were called Christians first at Antioch.

Acts 11:22-26

Barnabas and Paul—

[1]After this, Paul left Athens and went to Corinth. [2]There he met a Jew named Aquila, a native of Pontus, who had recently come from Italy with his wife Priscilla, because Claudius had ordered all the Jews to leave Rome. Paul went to see them, [3]and because he was a tentmaker as they were, he stayed and worked with them. . . .

[18]Paul stayed on in Corinth for some time. Then he left the brothers and sailed for Syria, accompanied by Priscilla and Aquila. . . .

Acts 18:1-3, 18

[3]Greet Priscilla and Aquila, my fellow workers in Christ Jesus. [4]They risked their lives for me. Not only I but all the churches of the Gentiles are grateful to them.

Romans 16:3-4

Paul, Priscilla, and Aquila—

[24]Meanwhile a Jew named Apollos, a native of Alexandria, came to Ephesus. He was a learned man, with a thorough knowledge of the Scriptures. [25]He had been instructed in the way of the Lord, and he spoke with great fervor and taught about Jesus accurately, though he knew only the

baptism of John. [26]He began to speak boldly in the synagogue. When Priscilla and Aquila heard him, they invited him to their home and explained to him the way of God more adequately.

Acts 18:24-26

Priscilla, Aquila, and Apollos—

How do these qualities apply to your current friendships?

Jesus As a Model for Friendship

Read the following passages and discuss the questions below:

[11]Mary stood outside the tomb crying. . . .

[14]At this, she turned around and saw Jesus standing there, but she did not realize that it was Jesus.

[15]"Woman," He said, "why are you crying? Who is it you are looking for?"

Thinking He was the gardener, she said, "Sir, if You have carried Him away, tell me where You have put Him, and I will get Him."

[16]Jesus said to her, "Mary."

She turned toward Him and cried out in Aramaic, "Rabboni!" (which means Teacher).

John 20:11, 14-16

Jesus and Mary Magdalene—

[38]As Jesus and His disciples were on their way, He came to a village where a woman named Martha opened her

home to Him. [39]She had a sister called Mary, who sat at the Lord's feet listening to what He said. [40]But Martha was distracted by all the preparations that had to be made. She came to Him and asked, "Lord, don't You care that my sister has left me to do the work by myself? Tell her to help me!"

[41]"Martha, Martha," the Lord answered, "you are worried and upset about many things, [42]but only one thing is needed. Mary has chosen what is better, and it will not be taken away from her."

Luke 10:38-42

[1]Now a man named Lazarus was sick. He was from Bethany, the village of Mary and her sister Martha. [2]This Mary, whose brother Lazarus now lay sick, was the same one who poured perfume on the Lord and wiped His feet with her hair. [3]So the sisters sent word to Jesus, "Lord, the one You love is sick."

[4]When He heard this, Jesus said, "This sickness will not end in death. No, it is for God's glory so that God's Son may be glorified through it." [5]Jesus loved Martha and her sister and Lazarus. . . .

[32]When Mary reached the place where Jesus was and saw Him, she fell at His feet and said, "Lord, if You had been here, my brother would not have died."

[33]When Jesus saw her weeping, and the Jews who had come along with her also weeping, He was deeply moved in spirit and troubled. [34]"Where have you laid him?" He asked.

"Come and see, Lord," they replied.

[35]Jesus wept. . . .

[38]Jesus, once more deeply moved, came to the tomb. It was a cave with a stone laid across the entrance. . . .

[43]Jesus called in a loud voice, "Lazarus, come out!" [44]The dead man came out, his hands and feet wrapped with

strips of linen, and a cloth around his face.

John 11:1-4, 32-35, 38, 43-44

Jesus, Mary, Martha, and Lazarus—

[21]Going on from there, He saw two other brothers, James son of Zebedee and his brother John. They were in a boat with their father Zebedee, preparing their nets. Jesus called them, [22]and immediately they left the boat and their father and followed Him.

Matthew 4:21-22

[51]As the time approached for Him to be taken up to heaven, Jesus resolutely set out for Jerusalem. [52]And He sent messengers on ahead, who went into a Samaritan village to get things ready for Him; [53]but the people there did not welcome Him, because He was heading for Jerusalem. [54]When the disciples James and John saw this, they asked, "Lord, do You want us to call fire down from heaven to destroy them?" [55]But Jesus turned and rebuked them, [56]and they went to another village.

Luke 9:51-56

Jesus and John—

[10]Then Simon Peter, who had a sword, drew it and struck the high priest's servant, cutting off his right ear. (The servant's name was Malchus.)

[11]Jesus commanded Peter, "Put your sword away! Shall I not drink the cup the Father has given Me?"

John 18:10-11

[54]Then seizing Him, they led Him away and took Him into the house of the high priest. Peter followed at a distance. [55]But when they had kindled a fire in the middle of the courtyard and had sat down together, Peter sat down with them. [56]A servant girl saw him seated there in the firelight.

She looked closely at him and said, "This man was with Him."

[57]But he denied it. "Woman, I don't know Him," he said.

[58]A little later someone else saw him and said, "You also are one of them."

"Man, I am not!" Peter replied.

[59]About an hour later another asserted, "Certainly this fellow was with Him, for he is a Galilean."

[60]Peter replied, "Man, I don't know what you're talking about!" Just as he was speaking, the rooster crowed. [61]The Lord turned and looked straight at Peter. Then Peter remembered the word the Lord had spoken to him: "Before the rooster crows today, you will disown Me three times." [62]And he went outside and wept bitterly.

Luke 22:54-62

[15]When they had finished eating, Jesus said to Simon Peter, "Simon son of John, do you truly love Me more than these?"

"Yes, Lord," he said, "You know that I love You."

Jesus said, "Feed My lambs."

[16]Again Jesus said, "Simon son of John, do you truly love Me?"

He answered, "Yes, Lord, You know that I love You."

Jesus said, "Take care of My sheep."

[17]The third time He said to him, "Simon son of John, do you love Me?"

Peter was hurt because Jesus asked him the third time, "Do you love Me?" He said, "Lord, You know all things; You know that I love You."

Jesus said, "Feed My sheep."

John 21:15-17

Jesus and Peter—

What are the special qualities in Jesus' intimate friendships?

Are there any particular insights you have gleaned as a result of looking at the interaction between Jesus and these intimate friends?

Do you note any difference in how Jesus interacted because of gender?

Do you think it is more difficult to maintain a friend of the same or opposite gender? Why?

How do you feel about having a friend of the opposite gender?

Why do you think Jesus did not have more than a few very close friends?

GROWING BY DOING

Personal Friendships and Boundaries

Take time to reflect on your current friendships. Make a friendship map by putting yourself in the center of the following space and placing your friends around you according to emotional closeness. Use circles for female and squares for males and write their names inside. Draw a line from you to each friend and write a short word or two that describes your relationship.

A person usually feels violated or disrespected when emotional boundaries are intruded. A boundary is an imaginary line that differentiates you from another person and allows you to feel separate enough to connect with others in an interdependent way. When a person is overly connected and dependent on you, or at the other extreme, distant and removed from you, you may feel dissatisfied with the relationship. Be aware of any boundaries that are not well defined for you with any particular friend and indicate it on your friendship map with an **X.**

Boundaries in Friendship

Boundaries are appropriate in all relationships, but each person may have a different tolerance for what is personally acceptable. Indicate your own personal preferences for boundary keeping with the same and opposite gender friendships in the following categories:

Intellectual

Emotional

Physical

Spiritual

What are two guidelines you would agree are important boundaries in your personal relationships with males and females in each of the categories just discussed?

GOING THE SECOND MILE

How to Be a Better Friend

Consider once again the example of Jesus in His response to friends. How would you like to be more loving or more confrontational to a particular friend. Imagine that your friend is here to listen to what you have to say. Imagine speaking a truth in love, sharing more about yourself, talking about a fuzzy boundary, or expressing an intimate feeling to that friend. Say what you need to say, and then take some time to hear your friend respond to what you've said. Let that imaginary conversation go back and forth for a while.

Now, pray for this friend and ask God for the ability to follow through this week with a behavior or verbal message that will enhance that friendship.

FOUR

Christian Mothering and Fathering

GroupSpeak: *"I was amazed at the amount of influence parents have on children's perceptions of themselves as male or female. As I learn more about what God has said about gender differences, I wonder what message I'm giving to children about what it means to be masculine or feminine. Now I feel that I can learn a lot about parenting by experiencing being God's child, and treating children as God treats me."*

Mothering and Fathering

An important part of who we are as a male or female is a result of how we experienced mothering and fathering in our formative years. The results of how we were parented don't end there, however, for maleness and femaleness is reproduced! We aren't speaking merely of biological reproduction, but of the fact that learning to be a male or female is socially reproduced. The most important reproducers of gender roles are parents.

Our children learn what it means to be a male or female by *observing* us. Much of gender role learning is caught and not taught. By our very actions we *model* what it means to be a female or a male to our children.

GETTING ACQUAINTED

When You Were a Child
Thinking back upon your childhood, reflect upon the relationship between yourself and your mother and father. In the spaces provided below, give five one-word descriptions for each of these relationships.

Mother's Relationship	*Father's Relationship*
__________	__________
__________	__________
__________	__________
__________	__________
__________	__________

If one thing could have been different in your relationship with your mother and father, what would it be?

With my mother

With my father

When You Are a Parent
In thinking of how you are a parent or how you would be (if you're not now a parent), complete the following sentences:

One thing I like about myself as a parent is

One thing I want to be better at as a parent is

GAINING INSIGHT

Understanding God As Parent

What better model for Christians to follow than that of God as parent. What is God like as a parent? By gaining an understanding of how God parents, we can begin to build a better biblical basis for human fathering and mothering. The Bible has much to say about the relationship between God and His children.

Try to construct an image of God as parent by recalling the many biblical references to God as parent. The following verses will give you a start in your understanding. Write down a few words or phrases that clarify your image of God as a parent after each passage.

[8]Then God said to Noah and to his sons with him: [9]"I now establish My covenant with you and with your descendants after you [10]and with every living creature that was with you—every living creature on earth. [11]I establish My covenant with you: Never again will all life be cut off by the waters of a flood; never again will there be a flood to destroy the earth."

[12]And God said, "This is the sign of the covenant I am making between Me and you and every living creature with you, a covenant for all generations to come: [13]I have set My rainbow in the clouds, and it will be the sign of the covenant between Me and the earth."

Genesis 9:8-13

[11]My son, do not despise the LORD's discipline and do not resent his rebuke, [12]because the LORD disciplines those He loves, as a father the son he delights in.

Proverbs 3:11-12

[37][Jesus said] "O Jerusalem, Jerusalem, you who kill the prophets and stone those sent to you, how often I have longed to gather your children together, as a hen gathers her chicks under her wings, but you were not willing."

Matthew 23:37

[14]For if you forgive men when they sin against you, your heavenly Father will also forgive you. . . . [26]Look at the birds of the air; they do not sow or reap or store away in barns, and yet your heavenly Father feeds them. Are you not much more valuable than they?

Matthew 6:14, 26

[5]A father to the fatherless, a defender of widows, is God in His holy dwelling.

Psalm 68:5

[16]For God so loved the world that He gave His one and only Son, that whoever believes in Him shall not perish but have eternal life.

John 3:16

[7]Cast all your anxiety on Him because He cares for you.

1 Peter 5:7

[3]At one time we too were foolish, disobedient, deceived and enslaved by all kinds of passions and pleasures. We lived in malice and envy, being hated and hating one another. [4]But when the kindness and love of God our Savior appeared, [5]He saved us, not because of righteous things we had done, but because of His mercy. He saved us through the washing of rebirth and renewal by the Holy Spirit, [6]whom He poured

out on us generously through Jesus Christ our Savior, [7]so that, having been justified by His grace, we might become heirs having the hope of eternal life.

Titus 3:3-7

[15]For we do not have a high priest who is unable to sympathize with our weaknesses, but we have one who has been tempted in every way, just as we are—yet was without sin.

Hebrews 4:15

GROWING BY DOING

Parenting Tasks

Mothers and fathers can be involved in many different ways in the lives of their children. Following is a list of eight different parenting tasks. If you have children, who performs each of the following tasks in your home? Simply put an **X** under either **Mainly Wife, Shared Equally,** or **Mainly Husband** for each task. If you are a single parent or do not have children, answer as you think you would share the task.

	Mainly Wife	Shared Equally	Mainly Husband
Administers discipline			
Changes diapers			
Coordinates children's schedule (music lessons, sports, visiting friends)			
Cares for the children (dresses, feeds, bathes, etc.)			
Gives attention to their spiritual growth and development			
Listens to their problems when they are hurting			
Manages the children's needs (buys clothes, handles doctor visits, etc.)			
Plays with the children			

GOING THE SECOND MILE

Sentence Completion
Complete the following sentences.
The one area in which I would like my spouse to be more involved as a mother/father to our children is

The one area in which I would like to become more involved myself as a mother/father to my children is

MACHO
LIB
JUST DO IT!
GAY
AIDS
ERA

FIVE

Sexuality and Gender

GroupSpeak: *"I wondered how sexuality could be a good gift from God when I saw so many Christians struggling in this area of their lives, and so few in the church willing to talk openly about the struggles of sexuality. Now I see that Scripture presents a positive, person-centered sexuality as the norm. I can use this to help me affirm my self-image, and to sort out the various messages I've received about my gender and sexuality."*

Created As Sexual Beings

We are created as sexual beings and it is pronounced good by our Creator. Why, then, do we have such difficulty acknowledging that our sexuality is a wonderful gift from God? One reason is that each of us struggles with what it means to be a sexual person.

None of us is immune from the struggle, for we have all experienced brokenness and disappointment in this area of our lives. Denying that we are sexual beings or attempting to separate our sexual selves from the totality of who we are leads to a further distortion. This keeps us from being the integrated persons God intends us to be.

Our focus this session is to affirm ourselves as sexual persons. We will examine the messages we receive about sexuality and our body image from family, friends, church, and society and compare this with a biblical perspective. We will consider some normative principles of sexual expression and decide how to make responsible decisions about our behavior. Gender influences on our sexuality will be a theme throughout, since sexuality is one important way to understand what it means to be created male and female.

GETTING ACQUAINTED

Messages About Sexuality
What messages have you received about your sexuality from the following sources?

Church

Home

Friends

Society

How do you think these messages affected your view of yourself as a sexual person? Were there any gender differences in the messages given/received?

Affirmation of Body Self-Image
Our sexuality is both affirmed and refuted through attitudes we receive about our bodies. In fact, the way we feel about our bodies tends to reflect the way we feel about ourselves. This section is for you alone and will not be shared with others unless you choose to do so.

First, write down the childhood messages you received about your body from:

Your Father

Your Mother

Your Siblings

Your Grandparents/Aunts/Uncles

Your Friends

Now, compare and contrast what was said or done that made you feel ashamed or embarrassed about your body with what was said or done that made you feel especially good and affirmed about your body. What were the specific incidents and/or behaviors that contributed to this? How have you been personally impacted by these messages?

GAINING INSIGHT

Scripture Study
Read the following passages from the Song of Songs.

[1]Solomon's Song of Songs. [2]Let him kiss me with the kisses of his mouth—for your love is more delightful than wine. [3]Pleasing is the fragrance of your perfumes; your name is like perfume poured out. No wonder the maidens love you! [4]Take me away with you—let us hurry! Let the king bring me into his chambers.

We rejoice and delight in you; we will praise your love more than wine.

How right they are to adore you! [5]Dark am I, yet lovely, O daughters of Jerusalem, dark like the tents of Kedar, like the tent curtains of Solomon. . . .

[9]I liken you, my darling, to a mare harnessed to one of the chariots of Pharaoh. [10]Your cheeks are beautiful with earrings, your neck with strings of jewels. [11]We will make you earrings of gold, studded with silver.

[12]While the king was at his table, my perfume spread its fragrance. [13]My lover is to me a sachet of myrrh resting between my breasts. [14]My lover is to me a cluster of henna blossoms from the vineyards of En Gedi.

[15]How beautiful you are, my darling! Oh, how beautiful! Your eyes are doves.

[16]How handsome you are, my lover! Oh, how charming! And our bed is verdant.

Song of Songs 1:1-5, 9-16

[1]How beautiful you are, my darling! Oh, how beautiful! Your eyes behind your veil are doves. Your hair is like a flock of goats descending from Mount Gilead. [2]Your teeth are like a flock of sheep just shorn, coming up from the washing. Each has its twin; not one of them is alone. [3]Your lips are like a scarlet ribbon; your mouth is lovely. Your temples behind your veil are like the halves of a pomegranate. [4]Your neck is like the tower of David, built with elegance; on it hang a thousand shields, all of them shields of warriors. [5]Your two breasts are like two fawns, like twin fawns of a gazelle that browse among the lilies. [6]Until the day breaks and the shadows flee, I will go to the mountain of myrrh and to the hill of incense. [7]All beautiful you are, my darling; there is no flaw in you. . . .

[11]Your lips drop sweetness as the honeycomb, my bride; milk and honey are under your tongue. The fragrance of your garments is like that of Lebanon. [12]You are a garden locked up, my sister, my bride; you are a spring enclosed, a sealed fountain.

Song of Songs 4:1-7, 11-12

[10]My lover is radiant and ruddy, outstanding among ten thousand. [11]His head is purest gold; his hair is wavy and black as a raven. [12]His eyes are like doves by the water streams, washed in milk, mounted like jewels. [13]His cheeks are like beds of spice yielding perfume. His lips are like lilies dripping with myrrh. [14]His arms are rods of gold set with chrysolite. His body is like polished ivory decorated with sapphires. [15]His legs are pillars of marble set on bases of pure gold. His appearance is like Lebanon, choice as its cedars. [16]His mouth is sweetness itself; he is altogether lovely. This is my lover, this my friend, O daughters of Jerusalem.

Song of Songs 5:10-16

[1]How beautiful your sandaled feet, O prince's daughter! Your graceful legs are like jewels, the work of a craftsman's hands. [2]Your navel is a rounded goblet that never lacks blended wine. Your waist is a mound of wheat encircled by lilies. [3]Your breasts are like two fawns, twins of a gazelle. [4]Your neck is like an ivory tower. Your eyes are the pools of Heshbon by the gate of Bath Rabbim. Your nose is like the tower of Lebanon looking toward Damascus. [5]Your head crowns you like Mount Carmel. Your hair is like royal tapestry; the king is held captive by its tresses. [6]How beautiful you are and how pleasing, O love, with your delights! [7]Your stature is like that of the palm, and your breasts like clusters of fruit. [8]I said, "I will climb the palm tree; I will take hold of its fruit." May your breasts be like the clusters of the vine, the fragrance of your breath like apples, [9]and your mouth like the best wine.

Song of Songs 7:1-9

Make a list of the attitudes expressed in these verses about various body parts and sexual expression.

What insights does your list give about sexuality and personhood?

In Song of Songs 7:10 the beloved says, "I belong to my lover, and his desire is for me." What does this statement mean to you?

Genesis 2:25 says that Adam and Eve were naked and not ashamed. What do you make of this? What do you think naked refers to?

Read the following verses.

[3]The husband should fulfill his marital duty to his wife, and likewise the wife to her husband. [4]The wife's body does not belong to her alone but also to her husband. In the same way, the husband's body does not belong to him alone but also to his wife. [5]Do not deprive each other except by mutual consent and for a time, so that you may devote yourselves to prayer. Then come together again so that Satan will not tempt you because of your lack of self-control.

1 Corinthians 7:3-5

How is gender equality addressed in this passage?

Normative Principles for Sexual Expression

Lewis Smedes, in his book, *Sex for Christians* (Eerdmans), lists the following normative principles of sexuality:

- ❑ Human sexuality ought to be integrated into the total development of a person's character.

- ❑ Human sexuality ought to tend toward expression in personal relationships.

- ❑ Human sexuality ought to drive us toward permanent heterosexual union.

Consider the wisdom of these statements in terms of your relationships with others. Do you find these standards helpful in making decisions about sexual expression today? Why or why not?

How do you deal with differences between these values and current attitudes and behaviors about sexual expression in today's society?

Making Decisions About Sexual Expression
Do you agree with the scriptural principle that all things are allowable for a person, but all things are not good? What would this mean in terms of making decisions about sexual expression?

What are some specific guidelines that would help you meet person-centered goals in your sexual involvement with others?

Why is it important for persons to believe they have the right to set boundaries and say no?

GROWING BY DOING

Growing Up the Opposite Gender
Have you ever imagined what it might be like to grow up the opposite gender? Have you ever wondered what your life

might be like today if you were male instead of female or female instead of male? In the next few minutes you will have that opportunity. Your leader will help you relax and reflect on this thought by leading you through an experience that helps you imagine what it would be like to be born the other gender. You will be guided through each stage of normal development from birth to adulthood. Be especially aware of gender differences in sexual awareness. This exercise will help you discover more about what it feels like to members of the opposite gender.

Take a few moments to ponder this experience. What was it like for you?

Did anything in particular surprise you?

What were the good things about being this gender? What were the difficult things for you?

Now, get with one other person to share your personal response to the exercise. Take time to listen to each other and talk about anything that you would like to share.

GOING THE SECOND MILE

Living As a Sexual Person
Everyone has sexual/gender struggles. We all falter in living out a consistent and integrated existence as men and women. There is none that is righteous, *no not one!* This is a time to renew, to consider how to be more faithful to scriptural and personal values in order to live out a positive, person-centered existence as sexual persons. Take some time to confess failures and ask for forgiveness and restoration. Recommit yourself toward that end in prayer.

Take the next few days to list some specific ways in which you will be more affirming of yourself and others as sexual persons. Indicate the guidelines you will apply to your own life in order to make person-centered, responsible decisions about your sexual interactions with others.

SIX

Where Is the Spouse I Thought I Married?

GroupSpeak: *"There was a time when it was clearly understood what husbands and wives were to do; in marriage today, everything seems to be up for grabs. Now I'm becoming aware that I've had some pretty traditional expectations in my relationships. This study has inspired me to explore ways that my partner and I can empower each other to be all that God wants us each to be."*

Supermen and Superwomen

The redefinition of gender roles is causing confusion and disruption between many married couples as they attempt to sort out their roles as husbands and wives. Females have traditionally acquired status by investing themselves in the task of being superwives and supermothers. Males, on the other hand, have acquired status by way of achievement in the workplace, usually validated by promotions and large salaries.

This situation is rapidly changing, however, as women increasingly assume responsibilities outside the home, particularly in the work force. Many women experience contradictory expectations between being the superwife and being a success outside the home. TV and other media adds to the confusion by encouraging romance, marriage, and childbearing while glorifying the independent, career-oriented woman.

The challenge for men is how to become more involved in the home, especially as fathers to their children, while at the same time fulfilling the demands called for in their job away from home. Feeling the opposing pull from work and family, many men come to feel frustrated because they don't see how they can do it all.

The media message given to women is that they must have it all! In an effort to do it all, they become superwomen who suffer stress and frustration. Whereas a husband may encourage his wife to do it all, he often does not pick up the slack in the home, so the woman is left with a double-duty workload. The result has been confusion and disruption in the marriage relationship. This can be especially true of middle-aged couples who began marriage when gender roles were more clearly defined. Changes in the husbands' and wives' roles have caused many a partner to wonder, "Where is the spouse I thought I married?"

GETTING ACQUAINTED

Do Opposites Attract?

Do "likes marry likes," or do "opposites attract"? Some couples will tell you that their marriages are strong because they are based upon important ways in which they are alike. Others will tell you that it is the ways in which they are different that strengthen their marriages. In reality, most couples are both alike and different in important ways.

List the five most important ways in which you and your spouse are alike and different. If you are not married, list the ways in which your "ideal" spouse would be alike and different from you.

Alike	**Different**
1. ______________	1. ______________
2. ______________	2. ______________
3. ______________	3. ______________
4. ______________	4. ______________
5. ______________	5. ______________

GAINING INSIGHT

Traditional Vs. Modern Marital Roles

Due to gender role changes there is currently a battle going on between those who defend *traditional* marital roles and those who argue for a *modern* view of marital roles. Those who defend the traditional proclaim the 19th-century patriarchal marriage as God's ideal. Those who argue in favor of the modern marriage seem willing to adapt marriage to "fit" in with the latest fad and innovation. The major differences between traditional and modern marital roles are summarized in the following chart.

CHARACTERISTICS OF THE TRADITIONAL AND MODERN MARRIAGE

TRADITIONAL	BIBLICAL IDEAL	MODERN
	Marital Commitment	
Commitment to marriage as an institution		Contract (self-fulfillment)
Coercive		Disengaged
Dutiful Sex (male pleasure)		Self-Centered Sex (personal pleasure)
	Marital Roles and Adaptability	
Law		Anarchy
Predetermined (role segregation)		Undetermined (undifferentiated roles)
Rigid/Stilted		Chaotic

Marital Authority

Ascribed Power	Possessive Power
Authoritarian male headship	No Authority (neither submissive)
Male Centered	Self Centered

Marital Communication

Inexpressiveness	Pseudo-Intimacy
Pronouncement (legislate)	Declaration (stalemate)
Nonassertive	Aggressive

A Christian Alternative

While it is true that the redefinition of gender roles has caused confusion in marriage relationships, current changes offer the opportunity to reexamine marital roles on the basis of a biblical ideal. As you examine each set of descriptions given by the **TRADITIONAL** and **MODERN** views of marriage, fill in the middle column with a word or brief description of what you consider a biblical ideal marriage to be.

Marital Commitment—Study the following verses.

[18]But I will establish My covenant with you, and you will enter the ark—you and your sons and your wife and your sons' wives with you. . . .

[22]Noah did everything just as God commanded him.
Genesis 6:18, 22

[9]"I now establish My covenant with you and with your descendants after you [10]and with every living creature that was with you—the birds, the livestock and all the wild ani-

mals, all those that came out of the ark with you—every living creature on earth.

Genesis 9:9-10

[1]When Abram was ninety-nine years old, the LORD appeared to him and said, "I am God Almighty; walk before Me and be blameless. [2]I will confirm My covenant between Me and you and will greatly increase your numbers. [3]Abram fell facedown, and God said to him, [4]"As for Me, this is My covenant with you: You will be the father of many nations. [5]No longer will you be called Abram; your name will be Abraham, for I have made you a father of many nations. [6]I will make you very fruitful; I will make nations of you, and kings will come from you. [7]I will establish My covenant as an everlasting covenant between Me and you and your descendants after you for the generations to come, to be your God and the God of your descendants after you.

Genesis 17:1-7

Marital Roles and Adaptability Although there are few Bible verses which specifically deal with marital roles, Scripture does teach that everything ought to be done with a sense of order and harmony, consideration and love. Read the following passages.

[9]Love must be sincere. Hate what is evil; cling to what is good. [10]Be devoted to one another in brotherly love. Honor one another above yourselves. [11]Never be lacking in zeal, but keep your spiritual fervor, serving the Lord. [12]Be joyful in hope, patient in affliction, faithful in prayer. [13]Share with God's people who are in need. Practice hospitality.

[14]Bless those who persecute you; bless and do not curse. [15]Rejoice with those who rejoice; mourn with those who mourn. [16]Live in harmony with one another. Do not be proud, but be willing to associate with people of low position. Do not be conceited.

[17]Do not repay anyone evil for evil. Be careful to do what is right in the eyes of everybody. [18]If it is possible, as far as it depends on you, live at peace with everyone.

Romans 12:9-17

[8]Finally, all of you, live in harmony with one another; be sympathetic, love as brothers, be compassionate and humble. [9]Do not repay evil with evil or insult with insult, but with blessing, because to this you were called so that you may inherit a blessing.

1 Peter 3:8-9

Based on your reading of these passages, what concept might best express the basis for marital roles and adaptability in a biblically ideal marriage?

Marital Authority Read the following familiar passage.

[21]Submit to one another out of reverence for Christ.

[22]Wives, submit to your husbands as to the Lord. [23]For the husband is the head of the wife as Christ is the head of the church, His body, of which He is the Savior. [24]Now as the church submits to Christ, so also wives should submit to their husbands in everything.

[25]Husbands, love your wives, just as Christ loved the church and gave Himself up for her [26]to make her holy, cleansing her by the washing with water through the word, [27]and to present her to Himself as a radiant church, without stain or wrinkle or any other blemish, but holy and blameless.

Ephesians 5:21-27

Based on your reading of these verses, what concept might best express the basis for marital authority in a biblically ideal marriage?

Marital Communication John gives us insights on how to communicate honestly. Read the following passage.

[16]And so we know and rely on the love God has for us.

God is love. Whoever lives in love lives in God, and God in him. [17]In this way, love is made complete among us so that we will have confidence on the day of judgment, because in this world we are like Him. [18]There is no fear in love. But perfect love drives out fear, because fear has to do with punishment. The one who fears is not made perfect in love.

[19]We love because He first loved us.

1 John 4:16-19

Based on your reading of these verses, what concept might best express the basis for marital communication in a biblically ideal marriage?

GROWING BY DOING

Complete the Statement

As you have attempted to construct a biblical ideal description of marriage, you may find that some of the traditional views and some of the modern views are in part approximate to that ideal. Completing the following statements will help you identify the positive and negative aspects of traditional and modern marriage forms.

As a woman/man the aspect of *traditional* marriage which is most positive is

The aspect I find most negative in the *traditional* view is

As a woman/man the aspect of *modern* marriage which I find most positive is

The aspect I find most negative in the *modern* view is

GOING THE SECOND MILE

Talking Ideals
Compare your biblical ideal with your spouse's biblical ideal on one of the four aspects of marriage presented in the comparison chart. With your spouse, try to think of ways in which you can better fulfill that ideal in your relationship with each other.

For example, if you choose to concentrate on *marital authority,* you may wish to list the ways which you can empower your spouse, the ways in which you experience your spouse empowering you, and the ways in which you need further empowering from your spouse. If you are single, identify your relational needs which can best be met by a member of the opposite gender.

Second, make a list of persons of the opposite gender for whom you feel a sense of trust.

SEVEN

My Boss Is a Woman! My Boss Is a Man!

GroupSpeak: *"We all had different experiences to share. I never before thought about the distinctions of what work might mean for women and for men. It was neat that we were able to help each other understand that God values the diversity of persons and kinds of work."*

Gender in the Workplace
Almost everyone has worked at some time outside the home. Gender is an important issue in work relationships. Some of the effects of gender are evident immediately; others are not as obvious and must be looked for, or they may end up being the unrecognized cause of a variety of job (and life!) stresses.

GETTING ACQUAINTED

Who's the Boss?
Get together with another group member that you feel comfortable with, but haven't spent much time with in the group. Describe the person you work for, or someone you have worked for in the past. Were they male or female? In what ways do/did you see them as leaders? Would you be more comfortable having a woman or a man as a boss? Why?

GAINING INSIGHT

Scripture Study

Proverbs 31:10-31 is often cited as a passage of Scripture extolling the virtuous housewife. However, it has some very nontraditional elements. Notice those elements as you read the passage.

[10]A wife of noble character who can find? She is worth far more than rubies. [11]Her husband has full confidence in her and lacks nothing of value. [12]She brings him good, not harm, all the days of her life. [13]She selects wool and flax and works with eager hands. [14]She is like the merchant ships, bringing her food from afar. [15]She gets up while it is still dark; she provides food for her family and portions for her servant girls. [16]She considers a field and buys it; out of her earnings she plants a vineyard. [17]She sets about her work vigorously; her arms are strong for her tasks. [18]She sees that her trading is profitable, and her lamp does not go out at night. [19]In her hand she holds the distaff and grasps the spindle with her fingers. [20]She opens her arms to the poor and extends her hands to the needy. [21]When it snows, she has no fear for her household; for all of them are clothed in scarlet. [22]She makes coverings for her bed; she is clothed in fine linen and purple. [23]Her husband is respected at the city gate, where he takes his seat among the elders of the land. [24]She makes linen garments and sells them, and supplies the merchants with sashes. [25]She is clothed with strength and dignity; she can laugh at the days to come. [26]She speaks with wisdom, and faithful instruction is on her tongue. [27]She watches over the affairs of her household and does not eat the bread of idleness. [28]Her children arise and call her blessed; her husband also, and he praises her: [29]"Many women do noble things, but you surpass them all." [30]Charm is deceptive, and beauty is fleeting; but a woman who fears the LORD is to be praised. [31]Give her the reward she has earned, and let her works bring her praise at the city gate.

Proverbs 31:10-31

What nontraditional characteristics of women do you find in this passage?

Is there an equivalent passage in Scripture about men? Consider the instructions to overseers and deacons in 1 Timothy.

[1]Here is a trustworthy saying: If anyone sets his heart on being an overseer, he desires a noble task. [2]Now the overseer must be above reproach, the husband of but one wife, temperate, self-controlled, respectable, hospitable, able to teach, [3]not given to drunkenness, not violent but gentle, not quarrelsome, not a lover of money. [4]He must manage his own family well and see that his children obey him with proper respect. [5](If anyone does not know how to manage his own family, how can he take care of God's church?) [6]He must not be a recent convert, or he may become conceited and fall under the same judgment as the devil. [7]He must also have a good reputation with outsiders, so that he will not fall into disgrace and into the devil's trap.

[8]Deacons, likewise, are to be men worthy of respect, sincere, not indulging in much wine, and not pursuing dishonest gain. [9]They must keep hold of the deep truths of the faith with a clear conscience. [10]They must first be tested; and then if there is nothing against them, let them serve as deacons.

[11]In the same way, their wives are to be women worthy of respect, not malicious talkers but temperate and trustworthy in everything.

[12]A deacon must be the husband of but one wife and must manage his children and his household well. [13]Those who have served well gain an excellent standing and great assurance in their faith in Christ Jesus.

1 Timothy 3:1-13

What nontraditional characteristics of men do you find in this passage?

Now read both passages, reversing the genders. How does the reversal make you feel?

GROWING BY DOING

What Is Work?
What's your view on work? Do you view it as a ministry? Is it a punishment? Do you enjoy working or despise it?

Do you work well with your boss?

How is this relationship influenced by your gender and your boss' gender?

Finish the Story
After your **Group Leader** distributes the story to you, take five minutes to write an ending for it.

Compare your story with that of other group members. Are there differences?

Do male social structures determine how women work in the standard Western world workplace?

Do women have to become like men to succeed? (*Can they, even if they become like men, succeed?*)

Do men ever work in any stereotypically female workplaces in our culture?

Is there "female work"? Name some.

Do men adopt a workplace's organization, or do they tend to overlay a different organizational structure?

How do men know what to do in the workplace? Who are their mentors? Why are there so few mentors for women?

Why are most CEOs male while most spokespersons are female?

GOING THE SECOND MILE

Writing Assignment
Write a short psalm or praise prayer as if you were a member of the opposite gender. Give it to the **Group Leader** at the beginning of the next session.

Worship Symbol
Bring some sort of worship symbol or object which represents your investment in this group to the next session. It need not be a big thing, but some physical item which you will briefly explain to the group as having meaning for you.

Some examples might include:

- ❑ Lipstick which wasn't worn when a woman tried an experiment with stereotypes and felt the group supporting her.

- ❑ A note of appreciation written by someone for something done out of the ordinary.

- ❑ A dinner receipt for a meal which celebrated a victory over a nagging bad habit.

- ❑ A magazine ad showing a healthy relationship as a new goal.

Work Smarter

Try working "smarter" this week. Notice relationships at work. How do gender dynamics affect productivity? Notice the differing perceptions of men and women at work (e.g., Does a family picture mean something different if it is on a man's desk or a woman's?).

EIGHT

Gender and Spiritual Maturity

GroupSpeak: *"The variety of images that people had for God was amazing! I would never have thought of all those myself! And it would have never occurred to me that men might sin differently than women! I'm glad that we had the chance to worship together to confess our unity after seven weeks of seeing the uniqueness of men and women."*

Barriers to Holiness

Spirituality is often thought of as something special, extraordinary, occasional. However, there is a long tradition in the Christian community of spirituality as something which fills every moment of every day; that one can be spiritual while doing mundane things like washing clothes, tending gardens, fulfilling one's vocation. If so, then persons are not spiritual only in some religious part of themselves, but in their whole being, body, and soul—and this includes their gender.

In this session we will be looking at our ideas of spiritual maturity and some barriers to holiness which are magnified by our gender stereotypes. This session comes last so that we remember not to divorce our spiritual selves from God and forget all the other parts of our lives which have been discussed before!

GETTING ACQUAINTED

Common Definitions
Recall your most spiritual experience. From this experience, try to fill in the following blanks:

I experienced God as

My denomination thinks of spirituality as

Spirituality is

Is spirituality different from piety? Why do you say so?

How is spirituality more than a change of behavior?

Which of the following movie or TV titles best describes your relationship to God?

Gunfight at the OK Corral
Butch Cassidy and the Sundance Kid
"The Young and the Restless"
The Breakfast Club
"Father Knows Best"
Aliens
My Favorite Year
The Ten Commandments

GAINING INSIGHT

Models of Spirituality
Read about the following biblical characters who are models of spiritual discernment and maturity.

[13]During harvest time, three of the thirty chief men came down to David at the cave of Adullam, while a band of

Philistines was encamped in the Valley of Rephaim. [14]At that time David was in the stronghold, and the Philistine garrison was at Bethlehem. [15]David longed for water and said, "Oh, that someone would get me a drink of water from the well near the gate of Bethlehem!" [16]So the three mighty men broke through the Philistine lines, drew water from the well near the gate of Bethlehem and carried it back to David. But he refused to drink it; instead, he poured it out before the LORD. [17]"Far be it from me, O LORD, to do this!" he said. "Is it not the blood of men who went at the risk of their lives?" And David would not drink it.

2 Samuel 23:13-17

How did David show discernment?

[8]Before the spies lay down for the night, she went up on the roof [9]and said to them, "I know that the LORD has given this land to you and that a great fear of you has fallen on us, so that all who live in this country are melting in fear because of you. [10]We have heard how the LORD dried up the water of the Red Sea for you when you came out of Egypt, and what you did to Sihon and Og, the two kings of the Amorites east of the Jordan, whom you completely destroyed. [11]When we heard of it, our hearts melted and everyone's courage failed because of you, for the LORD your God is God in heaven above and on the earth below. [12]Now then, please swear to me by the LORD that you will show kindness to my family, because I have shown kindness to you. Give me a sure sign [13]that you will spare the lives of my father and mother, my brothers and sisters, and all who belong to them, and that you will save us from death."

[14]"Our lives for your lives!" the men assured her. "If you don't tell what we are doing, we will treat you kindly and faithfully when the LORD gives us the land."

Joshua 2:8-14

How did Rahab show discernment?

[7]After the LORD had said these things to Job, He said to Eliphaz the Temanite, "I am angry with you and your two friends, because you have not spoken of Me what is right, as My servant Job has. [8]So now take seven bulls and seven rams and go to My servant Job and sacrifice a burnt offering for yourselves. My servant Job will pray for you, and I will accept his prayer and not deal with you according to your folly. You have not spoken of Me what is right, as My servant Job has." [9]So Eliphaz the Temanite, Bildad the Shuhite and Zophar the Naamathite did what the LORD told them; and the LORD accepted Job's prayer.

Job 42:7-9

How did Job show discernment?

[9]Hathach went back and reported to Esther what Mordecai had said. [10]Then she instructed him to say to Mordecai, [11]"All the king's officials and the people of the royal provinces know that for any man or woman who approaches the king in the inner court without being summoned the king has but one law: that he be put to death. The only exception to this is for the king to extend the gold scepter to him and spare his life. But thirty days have passed since I was called to go to the king."

[12]When Esther's words were reported to Mordecai, [13]he sent back this answer: "Do not think that because you are in the king's house you alone of all the Jews will escape. [14]For if you remain silent at this time, relief and deliverance for the Jews will arise from another place, but you and your father's family will perish. And who knows but that you have come to royal position for such a time as this?"

[15]Then Esther sent this reply to Mordecai: [16]"Go, gather together all the Jews who are in Susa, and fast for me. Do not eat or drink for three days, night or day. I and my maids will fast as you do. When this is done, I will go to the king, even though it is against the law. And if I perish, I perish."

[17]So Mordecai went away and carried out all of Esther's instructions.

Esther 4:9-17

How did Esther show discernment?

Name some other people you think of as being spiritually mature.

People in the Bible	People You Know of	People You Know Personally

Are there similarities between these three groups of people? Differences? Do these people on occasion manifest any works of the flesh? Was it easier to recall people of one gender more than another?

Genesis 3 describes the results of disobedience on the lives of the man and the woman, and the curse on the ground and on the serpent resulting from the Fall. Read these verses and answer the questions.

[16]To the woman He said, "I will greatly increase your pains in childbearing; with pain you will give birth to children. Your desire will be for your husband, and he will rule over you."

[17]To Adam He said, "Because you listened to your wife and ate from the tree about which I commanded you, 'You must not eat of it,' Cursed is the ground because of you; through painful toil you will eat of it all the days of your life. [18]It will produce thorns and thistles for you, and you will eat the plants of the field. [19]By the sweat of your brow you

will eat your food until you return to the ground, since from it you were taken; for dust you are and to dust you will return."

Genesis 3:16-19

Is there such a thing as a typically male sin? A typically female sin?

Are spiritual qualities gender specific?

What are common stereotypes of spirituality for females and males?

Do males and females experience God in different ways? Do they relate to God differently?

How we understand the differences between male and female socialization is helpful when we try to understand sin and holiness. For example, are males in Western society brought up to be more prone to pride than females? Or are women and men equally guilty in this area? Our understanding of the nature of sin will determine how we approach this. Let's look at two possible models.

If we were to draw a diagram of sin and holiness in regard to one's self-concept, how would the two be related? One possibility is that sin and holiness would be opposites. It is often thought that men tend toward pride more easily than women, and that women tend to defer more easily than men. Women and men would both fall between the extremes, as in the model on page 87. We call this the Polar model because sin and holiness are like the poles of a magnet. In this model, Person A, who wants to grow in godliness, would want to move to the right, toward humility. There is no danger of becoming too humble, so the more to the right that Person A moves, the better.

SIN		Stereo-		Person		Stereo-		*HOLINESS*
Pride	→	typed	→	A	→	typed	→	Humility
Arrogance		Men				Women		Deference

If women are stereotypically more deferent, is it true that they start out being more godly than men? Does a man need to become more like a woman in order to become more holy? Do women need to become ever more deferential to become more godly? Is this "natural" holiness of women due to something in the nature of womanhood? Is a "natural" sinfulness of men due to the nature of manhood? Or are these assumptions related to how women and men have been socialized? These are the resulting questions we must deal with if we picture sin as the opposite pole of holiness.

Compare the Polar model with the following model where holiness is pictured as a target, and sin is understood as "missing the mark." We call this the Target model. The farther we are from the target in any direction, the farther from godliness we are. Person B may want to become more humble, but now there is a danger of overcompensation.

SIN		Stereo-		Person		*HOLINESS*		Stereo-		Person		*SIN*
Pride	→	typed	→	B	→	Humility	←	typed	←	C	←	Silence
Self-		men				Self-		women				Self-
promotion						assertion						negation

In this model, men do not need to become like women in order to be godly. Neither are women told to live a life of endless deference! If men are more prone to pride than women are, this is paralleled by women who are more prone to keep quiet, who fail to state the truth and defend it—whether that truth is the Gospel of Jesus Christ or the expression of their own needs and desires. In this model, women are not naturally holier than men. It is hard for men to resist the temptation toward excessive self-concept; it is just as hard for women to resist the temptation toward deficient self-concept. It seems that Jesus' temptations in the wilderness focused on these same themes. Trying pride first, Satan asked Jesus to turn stones into bread; that is, to use His divine power in an arrogant, self-serving way. Jesus refused. Then, turning to humility, Satan asked Jesus to throw Himself from the top of the temple; that is, to be completely dependent upon divine power and not act on His understanding of God. Again Jesus refused. Finally, Satan combined the two temptations and offered Jesus all the kingdoms of the world in exchange for worship; that is, glorification in exchange for deference. Jesus refused a third time. Jesus' actions reveal a center of holiness. And the Holy Spirit comes to conform us to that same Christlikeness.

GROWING BY DOING

Celebrate Your Gender
As the **Group Leader** collects and reads aloud the group's poems or prayers from Session 7's assignment, try to determine whether each item read was from the perspective of a woman or a man.

Because the image of God in human persons is so fundamentally social, it takes the Holy Spirit's work in and through community to help us become more Christlike. Therefore, this session is designed to reaffirm the social character of aid we have given each other in overcoming barriers to holiness.

In Session 7, we were asked to bring some gift or worship symbol to this session which represents what this study on gender has meant for us. Share your worship symbol or gift with the group. Remember, because the gift is your own response to God, it should express *your* feelings.

GOING THE SECOND MILE

Empowered by Prayer
Choose another person in the group and make a commitment to pray regularly for him or her. Tell the person that you will pray at least once a month that he or she will be empowered by the Holy Spirit to overcome cultural barriers to holiness and to celebrate the gift of gender.

DEAR SMALL GROUP LEADER:

Picture Yourself As A Leader.

List some words that describe what would excite you or scare you as a leader of your small group.

A Leader Is Not . . .

- ❑ a person with all the answers.
- ❑ responsible for everyone having a good time.
- ❑ someone who does all the talking.
- ❑ likely to do everything perfectly.

A Leader Is . . .

- ❑ someone who encourages and enables group members to discover insights and build relationships.
- ❑ a person who helps others meet their goals, enabling the group to fulfill its purpose.
- ❑ a protector to keep members from being attacked or taken advantage of.
- ❑ the person who structures group time and plans ahead.
- ❑ the facilitator who stimulates relationships and participation by asking questions.
- ❑ an affirmer, encourager, challenger.

- ❑ enthusiastic about the small group, about God's Word, and about discovering and growing.

What Is Important To Small Group Members?

- ❑ A leader who cares about them.
- ❑ Building relationships with other members.
- ❑ Seeing themselves grow.
- ❑ Belonging and having a place in the group.
- ❑ Feeling safe while being challenged.
- ❑ Having their reasons for joining a group fulfilled.

What Do You Do . . .

If nobody talks—

- ❑ Wait—show the group members you expect them to answer.
- ❑ Rephrase a question—give them time to think.
- ❑ Divide into subgroups so all participate.

If somebody talks too much—

- ❑ Avoid eye contact with him or her.
- ❑ Sit beside the person next time. It will be harder for him or her to talk sitting by the leader.
- ❑ Suggest, "Let's hear from someone else."
- ❑ Interrupt with, "Great! Anybody else?"

If people don't know the Bible—

- ❑ Print out the passage in the same translation and hand it out to save time searching for a passage.
- ❑ Use the same Bible versions and give page numbers.
- ❑ Ask enablers to sit next to those who may need encouragement in sharing.
- ❑ Begin using this book to teach them how to study; affirm their efforts.

If you have a difficult individual—

- ❑ Take control to protect the group, but recognize that exploring differences can be a learning experience.
- ❑ Sit next to that person.
- ❑ To avoid getting sidetracked or to protect another group member, you may need to interrupt, saying, "Not all of us feel that way."
- ❑ Pray for that person before the group meeting.

ONE

A Traditional Look at Women and Men

How can we successfully understand what it means to be created in the image of God as female and male? In order to pursue the theme of this study, we must first take a look at the traditional foundations of gender identity and the patterns and images based on those traditional gender stereotypes that we have incorporated into our own lives. Then, since most of our lives are also filled with images of women and men obtained from many media (TV, radio, books, magazines, movies) and non-media sources (church and civic organizations, work relationships, friends, and families), we will begin to examine the stereotype assumptions that we incorporate from these sources as well.

In this first session, group members will be wanting to know if this group is going to be fun and worth their time and effort. They'll be asking themselves if they belong and are wanted here, and what is expected of them. You'll want to help begin clarifying these things with them.

Your influence as the **Group Leader** will be high at the start of a small group. At this first meeting, you can summarize the kind of group *you* expect this to be, and your attitude will be catching!

Every small group needs the four **Cs**—some form of Commitment, absolute **C**onfidentiality, a **C**aring **C**limate, and **Con**tent—in order to grow together in Christ. We will say more about each of these in various ways throughout the eight sessions. You can help the small group be constructed to meet these needs.

As **Group Leader** of this small group experience, *you* have a choice as to which elements will best fit your group, your style of leadership, and your purposes. After you examine the **Session Objectives**, select the activities under each heading with which to begin your community building. You have many choices.

SESSION OBJECTIVES

- ✓ To be introduced to each other and begin to feel comfortable with the group.
- ✓ To discuss and draw up a group covenant or "commitment contract" that includes, but is not limited to, what the group wants to do together (content), what they want the group to feel like (climate), including especially trust (confidentiality), and what the self-chosen duties of each member are (commitment).
- ✓ To identify gender and personal character qualities.

GETTING ACQUAINTED 20–30 minutes

If your group is not well acquainted, take time at least to get to know one another's names before beginning this session. If the group is strong in its relational bonds, the following exercises may help to strengthen the group.

Have a group member read aloud **A Balanced Picture.** Then choose one of the following activities to help create a more comfortable, nonthreatening atmosphere for the first meeting of your small group.

Good Folk
Let the group members know that they should spend about 5 minutes on this section.

Kin Folk
Allow about 10–15 minutes for group members to complete their genograms. Then have group members share with each other some of the positive character quality traits of the people that they have chosen to list in the **Good Folk** and **Kin Folk** activities. Help them to see that these characteristics are *not* gender-bound. Girls as well as boys can be strong, gentle, patient, and courageous; and men as well as women show insight, obedience, determination, and compassion, among many other qualities.

If your group has trouble coming up with words, here are some possible traits to use as examples: active, affectionate, ambitious, assertive, brave, calm, careful, cheerful, clean, compassionate, confident, courteous, decisive, determined, disciplined, dominant, ethical, empathetic, emotional, faithful, friendly, gentle, generous, good, happy, helpful, humble, humorous, independent, insightful, integrity, intelligent, intuitive, joyful, kind, liberated, logical, loving, loyal, nice, obedient, open, patient, peaceful, rational, reasonable, responsible, reverent, risk-taker, self-controlled, self-reliant, sensible, serving, single-minded, sociable, steady, supportive, tactful, thoughtful, thrifty, true-blue, trustworthy, truthful, warm, well-balanced.

Your group will probably come up with a lot of these and other traits, and some will perhaps disagree on the necessary positiveness of each of them. This is to be expected and indicates that your group is beginning to grow its own identity. Use this time to reflect back to your group that it is OK, and in fact to be hoped for, that each of you will have different ideas to share. This is one of the signs of a healthy group.

Pocket Principle

1 **One of the things that will help to make your group gel is knowing that it is a safe place to discuss new ideas. To foster this, the group must be comfortable—the group is safe internally. Nothing shared in the group is disparaged or discarded. This is part of the caring context of the group, just like prayer and learning every-**

one's name is. And the group must be confidential—the group is safe externally. Nothing shared in the group will ever be shared outside the group, with anyone, including with you as the leader, or with any subset of the group.

Optional—Famous People Name Tags

In advance, write famous people's names on name tags, enough for the group plus a few extras. These can be characters from the Bible, fairy tales, politics, or local folk. Use both men's and women's names.

Explain that you are going to put a famous person's name on each person's back. Then, everyone is going to try to help everyone else guess who they are. The only rules are that they cannot ask or give the gender of the person until you give the OK to do so, and that they must be helpful in their responses without giving away the name. People should try to ask and answer "positive personal qualities and character traits" questions to discover who they are.

This is a cooperative game, designed to help everyone get acquainted, and begin thinking about character traits. No one wins this game and no one loses. People who discover who they are should stay in the game and help everyone else. About 5 minutes into the game, allow people to ask which gender their name tag person is, if needed.

After everyone has discovered who they are, ask: **What were the key elements that you needed in order to discover who you were? Was anyone able to figure out who they were without knowing their gender? Was anyone surprised to discover which gender their person was?**

Optional—Gender Benders

For this game, make enough copies of the following list for everyone in the group. Everyone will be attempting to find two other members of the group who do each of the items on the list. They should have each of those people sign their names on their list and attempt to get signatures for at least two items from each person in the group. If you don't use this game here, it could be used in Session 7. You may even want to use it *both* times, to see if there are any changes from the beginning to the end of the group meetings.

GENDER BENDERS

___ I wash dishes.
___ I contribute more than 20% of the family financial income.
___ I keep my own appointment calendar.
___ I change diapers.
___ I exercise regularly.
___ I balance a checkbook regularly.
___ I do laundry.
___ I work in the garden.
___ I purchase greeting/holiday cards myself.
___ I mow the lawn.
___ I am my own secretary.
___ I read the newspaper regularly.
___ I use some form of transportation to get to work.
___ I drop the children off at school/day care on my way to work.
___ I cook most of the meals in our family.
___ I write letters to my friends.

To spark group discussion after the game ask: **Are there any surprises in who signed what?** Have group members mark each item as either a male or female activity. Discuss why they think this. Ask: **What in our culture leads you to these responses?**

GAINING INSIGHT 20–25 minutes

Scripture Study
Here are some things you will need to know as you lead the group in discussing the questions about Genesis 1:26-27 and Galatians 5:22-23. We assume that women are created equal with men and share equally the image of God. They each are assigned the work of dominionover creation. They are of the

same essence. Genesis 1:26-27 presents God's creation of humankind, not focusing on whether one is a man or one is a woman.

Galatians 5 does not make any sexual differentiation in the fruit of the Spirit. This is also true of Romans 12 and 1 Corinthians 12. Paul makes no distinctions in reference to which gender bears which gifts.

Optional—One Word Descriptions
Have the group brainstorm for 10 minutes one-word descriptions of Jesus. Have them focus on traits/attributes of character, not on things like Jewish, male, Galilean, Son of God, etc. If people are having trouble finding words to describe Jesus, have them look at Philippians 2:1-18. Stop when ideas are dwindling.

Identify the traits as "male," "female," or "neutral." Ask: **What does this say about our societal stereotypes? Is Jesus more stereotypically male or female? Could Jesus be neutral or neither rather than one or the other of our stereotypes? It has been said that Jesus did not buy into nor perpetuate any stereotypes. Why should or do we?**

GROWING BY DOING 15–20 minutes

Sharing
This exercise may be scary because we're still a new group and we don't know each other well yet. And it is even harder sharing something fairly personal with only one other person than something less personal with the entire group. Remind group members that they don't need to share anything they don't want to share, but that sharing what they can makes the group a group!

GOING THE SECOND MILE 5 minutes

Media Exploration
Challenge your group members to do this research on their own. Next week both the ad and TV images will be looked at. You may want to bring several magazines to look through.

Ask group members to consider this question: **How are you a traditional representative of your stereotype?**

Consider having group members go back to someone who taught them how to be the gender they are and thank them for teaching them so well.

GROWING AS A LEADER

Group Checkup

By now you will have experienced the ups and downs of the first meeting of your small group. Probably, you will know a little bit more about each person in the group. List something here to pray about for each one this week.

Each of the group members is making refinements in what they hope for and expect from the group. Most likely, so are you! This is the beginning of a natural process for growing groups. During the course of the eight weeks, the group will grow closer, and it is important that the members become able to view the group as their group, rather than your group. You will be facilitating this process, by using your growing skills as a small group leader to help the small group grow in its maturity.

During the course of the small group, your position of responsibility as the up-front leader of the group will vary in its intensity and format. Other group members will exhibit various kinds of leadership skills at different times in the group, and you can encourage this as you become aware of the needs of the group. Your particular leadership responsibility is likely to vary from week to week from the beginning to the end of the study.

You have your own style, so the best way for you to be a good leader is to be yourself! These hints are simply to help you as you become a member of the group in a special way.

TWO

Liberated Men and Women

In this session, liberation is presented as the ability to overcome stereotypes. Jesus broke many stereotypes, as we saw in the exercise last week which used single words to describe Jesus. By noticing stereotypes, and understanding how they influence us, group members should have greater freedom to go outside the boundaries of their own stereotypes. But being aware may not be enough. So the issue of power is raised, and Jesus is presented as a model for breaking some stereotypes.

Going outside the boundaries of stereotypes requires personal strength, and Christianity ought to be a place where people can be "empowered" to do this. Looking to Jesus as an exceptional role model may well be the source of strength we need to begin experimenting with liberation!

As **Group Leader** of this small group experience, *you* have a choice as to which elements will best fit your group, your style of leadership, and your purposes. After you examine the **Session Objectives**, select the activities under each heading with which to begin your community building. You have many choices.

SESSION OBJECTIVES

- √ To get acquainted so we have a sense that we are not alone in our feelings of power and powerlessness.
- √ To become aware of stereotypes and the bondage that they place us in at times.
- √ To recognize the power and model available to us in Jesus to overcome this cultural bondage.
- √ To understand the sort of power which Jesus has to break stereotypes.
- √ To encourage each other to experiment in following Jesus' liberation.

GETTING ACQUAINTED 20–30 minutes

Have a group member read aloud **Liberated From What?** Then choose one of the following activities to help create a more comfortable, nonthreatening atmosphere.

The Power Line

Divide your meeting area into two sections: high-powered and low-powered. As you work through this activity, ask group members to indicate their level of power in each of the six spheres by moving to the appropriately designated area of the room. Tell them to feel free to stand at a midpoint if that is how they feel.

Instruct group members to take a moment to talk with the others who are standing near them. Ask: **Do you keep bumping into the same people? See if you share some of the same reasons for standing where you are. How do you feel about being in the place that you are in?**

After moving through the six spheres, call the whole group back together again for discussion concerning any patterns you noticed in people's movement from or to the place of power as they shifted spheres. You may notice that females tend to feel more powerful at school than in the family, or you might notice that people who feel powerless in one sphere feel powerless in all spheres. Note any gender differences, and ask if anyone found themselves as the only person of one gender in a group, and would they be willing to tell the whole group about that.

If you do not notice any patterns, you may want to ask: **Where would Jesus have stood regarding each of these spheres?** Another issue to raise is what it is like to have power and be in control. Ask: **When you felt powerful, did this power feel liberating (due to the freedom) or did it feel constricting (because of the responsibility), or perhaps neither of these? Are there different sorts of power? Name some. What sort of power did Jesus have?**

As a leader, you should be aware that some people only feel needed (and in a certain sense, powerful) when they are in a very sharply defined relationship, even if the relationship is difficult. This exercise may prove uncomfortable for such people. If this comes up, feel free to follow up on this with them at a later time. The whole group might think about the issue by trying to determine whether some types of power are unhealthy.

Optional—The As/So Pattern
Take a sheet of newsprint (or butcher paper) and ask a group member to read John 17:18.

[18]"As You sent Me into the world, I have sent them into the world."

John 17:18

Stop the person reading after he or she says, "As You sent Me" and ask the group to define how God sent Jesus into the world. Note their responses on your paper. Ask: **Was Jesus a member of the clergy? Did Jesus come in power? What sort of power did Jesus present?** After about 5–10 minutes of brainstorming, ask the reader to conclude the verse. Now spend another five minutes discussing how Christians are in the world. Ask: **What does this say about the sort of power we are to exercise?**

Optional—Purple Liberation
Read Jenny Joseph's poem, "Warning" (*When I Am An Old Woman, I Shall Wear Purple*, Papier-Maché Press, 1987). Discuss how the woman in this poem is being liberated. Ask: **Where does she stand in the spheres above? Where would Jesus encourage her or be a model for her?**

GAINING INSIGHT 20–30 minutes

Free From Stereotypes
Assign each group member one of the characters and passages in this section. After group members have determined what is unusual (or atypical) about their assigned characters, ask: **How do you respond to these characters and their actions? Did any of them sound odd to you? Are any of them attractive? Which person would you most like to be?**

Have each group member share the character they chose, whether it is possible for them to accomplish similar tasks, and why.

Ask a group member to read aloud Mark 10:42-45. Point out that Jesus' words seem to assume at least two types of persons with regard to power: the person who lords it over others, and the person who does not even aspire to power, who is a servant to all. We often add a third type, the person who uses power benevolently. When everyone has finished writing responses, discuss the following questions.

- ❑ **Jesus is describing a kind of relationship which employs power when He says, "Not so with you." Describe in your own words the relationship Jesus is opposing.** (Jesus is opposing a relationship where other people are the means to an end; where people manipulate other people; where there is a hierarchy of persons; where one relishes one's own power.)

- ❑ **Is what Jesus is opposing a barrier to holiness?** (Yes! All these are dehumanizing. Even hierarchical relations, while unavoidable in some sense [teacher-student], must always give way to the relationship of peers ["I no longer call you servants . . . I have called you friends," John 15:15].)

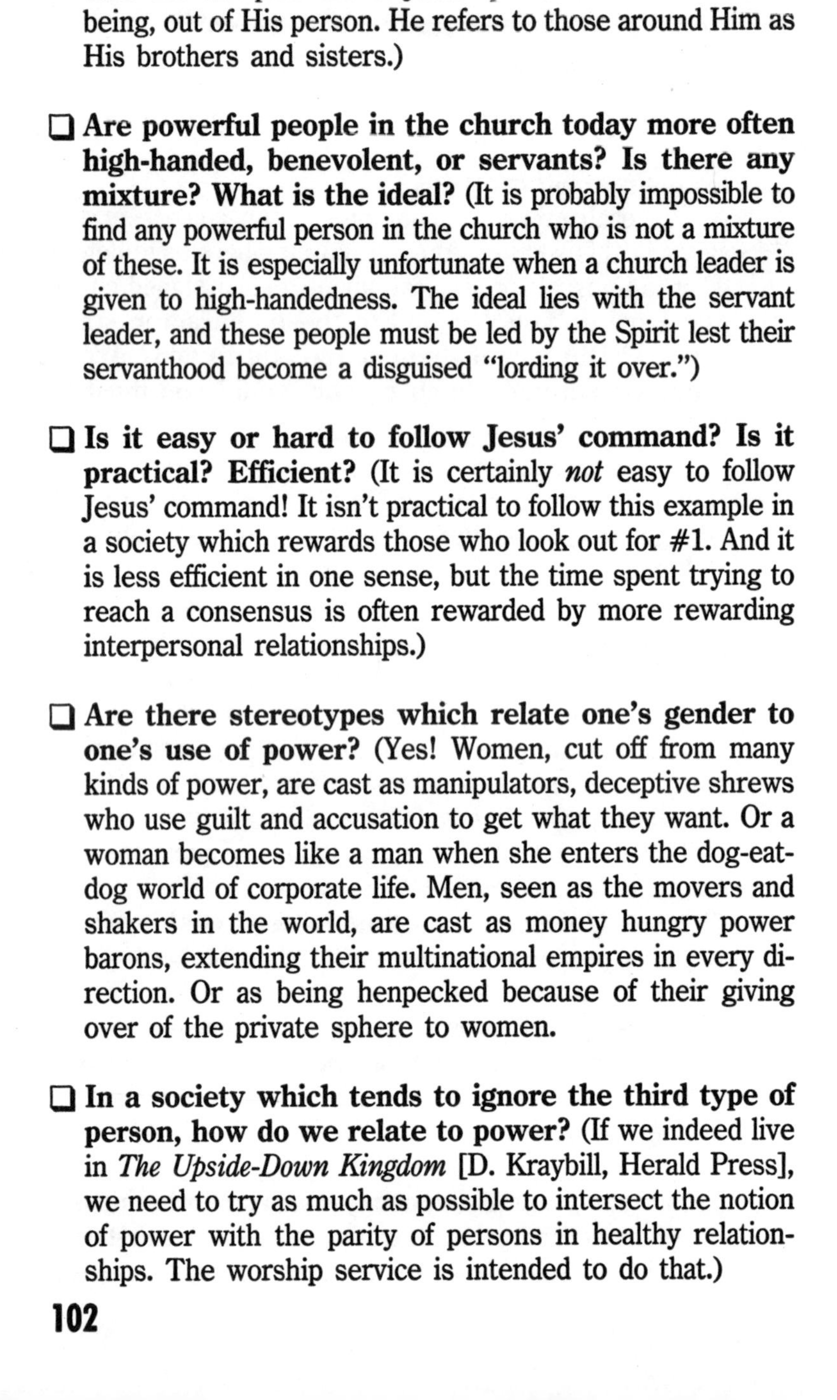

❑ **Which type of person is Jesus?** (Jesus does not lord it over the disciples. All of Jesus' power comes out of His being, out of His person. He refers to those around Him as His brothers and sisters.)

❑ **Are powerful people in the church today more often high-handed, benevolent, or servants? Is there any mixture? What is the ideal?** (It is probably impossible to find any powerful person in the church who is not a mixture of these. It is especially unfortunate when a church leader is given to high-handedness. The ideal lies with the servant leader, and these people must be led by the Spirit lest their servanthood become a disguised "lording it over.")

❑ **Is it easy or hard to follow Jesus' command? Is it practical? Efficient?** (It is certainly *not* easy to follow Jesus' command! It isn't practical to follow this example in a society which rewards those who look out for #1. And it is less efficient in one sense, but the time spent trying to reach a consensus is often rewarded by more rewarding interpersonal relationships.)

❑ **Are there stereotypes which relate one's gender to one's use of power?** (Yes! Women, cut off from many kinds of power, are cast as manipulators, deceptive shrews who use guilt and accusation to get what they want. Or a woman becomes like a man when she enters the dog-eat-dog world of corporate life. Men, seen as the movers and shakers in the world, are cast as money hungry power barons, extending their multinational empires in every direction. Or as being henpecked because of their giving over of the private sphere to women.

❑ **In a society which tends to ignore the third type of person, how do we relate to power?** (If we indeed live in *The Upside-Down Kingdom* [D. Kraybill, Herald Press], we need to try as much as possible to intersect the notion of power with the parity of persons in healthy relationships. The worship service is intended to do that.)

GROWING BY DOING

Stereotypes

Have the group brainstorm some contemporary models of powerful and competent behavior. Then discuss the stereotypes expressed in your group members' collections of ads, etc. Suggest the following:

The Wise Grandmother	The Rugged Outdoorsman
The Alluring Beauty	The Business Executive
The Old Battle-Axe	The Blundering Bachelor
The Dizzy Blond	The Don Juan

Ask: **Do you fit into one or more of these stereotypes? Do these feel limiting or restrictive? Are there any biblical persons who only fit into one stereotype? Does any person anywhere fit only one type? What good are stereotypes?**

Explain that often an ad will try to convey the idea that use of a particular product will attract romantic possibilities. Challenge the group to watch TV this week with an eye for how women relate to each other. Notice how often sex is used to sell something to men (e.g., an alluring beauty in a car or holding a particular kind of beer) and how often it is used to sell to women (a business executive who notices a woman wearing a particular perfume). Note that often a man pictured with one woman will be "distracted" by another woman who is using the advertised product. Encourage group members to keep track and report their findings at the next session.

Optional—Gender Change

Have group members pick a parable and change the gender of one of the people in the story. For example:

- ❑ Lazarus and the rich woman (Luke 16:19-31)
- ❑ the widower's offering (Mark 12:41-44)
- ❑ the Good Samaritan as a woman (Luke 10:25-37)
- ❑ the Prodigal Daughter (Luke 15:11-32)
- ❑ the persistent widower (18:1-8)

Discuss how the parable would have been different if it had happened with the opposite gender. Consider role-playing the parable, noting where it would have been different or similar with the gender changed. After acting out the parable, ask group members to express their reactions to anything which sounded odd to them and why they thought so. Ask: **Where do our stereotypes make it more difficult to "believe" the parable?**

Optional—Who Had More Power?
Have a volunteer read John 8. Ask: **Who had more power in the life of the woman caught in the act of adultery—the Pharisees or Jesus? Why didn't the crowd bring the man along as well?** (The crowd had the power of the Law to stone the woman; Jesus had the power of God to restore her.) **Which kind of power is most effective? Are all forms of power permissible for the Christian? Why or why not?** Describe for the whole group something you did which felt powerful to you which you think everyone else would approve of. Share any misuses of power as well.

GOING THE SECOND MILE

Freedom to Go Outside the Boundaries
This activity may be easier if you as a leader tell the group what atypical behavior you are going to try this week! Be sure to allow some brainstorming time for ideas!

Pocket Principle

1 **Liberation from stereotypes involves acting on a new strength and security. People in the group will now start probing how much they can trust each other. This is a good time to remind everyone of the pledge of confidentiality, and that they have agreed not to disclose to anyone anything about what is said or done in this small group. People rightly feel powerless if they cannot trust the other members of the group. If someone has spoken freely, things said within the group could be used against them unless the group is accountable to confidentiality! Everyone**

should promise to respect each person's thoughts and feelings without judging them. All doubts and questions are to be welcomed. No question can ever be heretical; only answers can be.

One understanding of liberation is freedom from the strict roles that society places upon people. Some of the questions in this section ask people to consider doing something "deviant" or "atypical." There will be a natural resistance to this and you will want to help them see the benefit of this exercise. Liberation is, in part, the ability to try something out of the ordinary. You will need to support those who do something unusual, noting that this is intended to be an experiment, and the resistance is part of the observation. Be sure everyone has fun!

GROWING AS A LEADER

Empowering Others

Notice who is doing the most talking in your group and find a way to encourage those who haven't had a chance to talk. Watch for the person who is trying to speak but is reluctant to jump in before the end of someone else's statement. If one group member is dominating the group's time, try sitting right next to him or her. Your nearness will often keep that person from forming a conversation with you. By your actions, you can empower those who are feeling powerless in the group.

THREE

Friendship and Gender

We are created in God's image by a relational God! The reference to "Us" and "Our" in Genesis 1:26 directs us to the relationship between the Persons of the Trinity. The Holy Trinity represents three distinct persons acting together in unity, thus the Three in One description. In Genesis 2, it is clear that God did not think it was good for a person to be alone, so He made another human being who corresponded and was complementary, indicating the social and relational nature of human life.

In the New Testament we are given the honor of being called friends of Christ when we do the will of God. Friendship is an important part of being created in relationship. Jesus models this through the relationships He established with both male and female friends in His earthly existence.

As **Group Leader** of this small group experience, *you* have a choice as to which elements will best fit your group, your style of leadership, and your purposes. After you examine the **Session Objectives**, select the activities under each heading with which to begin your community building. You have many choices.

SESSION OBJECTIVES

√ To consider relationships to both male and female friends.
√ To reflect on gender issues in order to make conscious decisions about establishing relationship with friends of both genders.
√ To look at Jesus as a model of being in relationship with friends of both genders.

GETTING ACQUAINTED 20–30 minutes

Have a group member read aloud **In His Image.** Then choose one of the following activities to help create a more comfortable, nonthreatening atmosphere.

Early Friendships
This activity is designed to have group members share about their early childhood friendships. It will help them recognize the importance of their early childhood friends and the influence these friends had in shaping attitudes about gender. Have each group member complete this section on their own.

Then take 10 minutes for group members to share something from their lists. Ask: **Do you notice any gender differences in the kinds of activities or expression of affection between friends?** Boys, for example, may have wrestled, whereas girls held hands as a way of showing affection.

Pocket Principle

1 **Be aware that questions about early memories may bring up painful experiences for some members. If anyone is reluctant to discuss or expresses anxiety about this exercise, don't pressure them to share in the larger group. Be sure to follow up sometime before the next meeting with that person, giving an opportuni-**

ty for further processing about any feelings that were stirred up.

My Special Friend
Divide the group into dyads or triads and provide each small group with paper and pens. Have each person focus on one particular childhood friend, drawing a picture of an activity that depicts their relationship. Triad/dyad group member(s) will try to guess the activity being drawn. Then spend a little time in more serious sharing why this friend/peer was so special.

Reassemble the group and ask volunteers to share anything they learned about themselves, friendships, and gender patterns as they looked at their childhood friendships. Ask: **Are there any specific patterns of interacting with same/opposite gender friends? Did anyone choose a friend of the opposite gender as their current special friend? Why or why not?**

GAINING INSIGHT 30–35 minutes

Understanding Friendship
These Scripture passages are meant to help group members reflect on important friendship dimensions between both same and opposite gender relationships, and to apply the qualities to their relationships with others.

Assign each group member one or more passages. Instruct group members to read the passages and list the qualities of these friendships. Take some time to share lists and discuss together whether they apply to current friendships.

Jesus As a Model of Friendship
This section gives the group a chance to discover how Jesus interacted with various friends in the Gospels. He established friendship with both genders and seemed comfortable doing so.

Break the group into four study teams so each can read one of the passages presented and make comments about these relationships. Then come together in the large group and share the findings of each section. List the qualities of these friendships, paying close attention to any differences in how Jesus related to different gender friends.

Point out that He initiated close friendships and received others' love and affection openly. He asked, "Peter, do you love Me?" He challenged, "She is doing the better thing, Martha." Friendship has to do with giving and receiving in mutual ways. Ask: **How does Jesus express intimacy with friends of the same and opposite gender?**

You may ask if there are any volunteers from the group who have had a good friend of the opposite gender and would talk about what was special as well as what was difficult about that friendship.

Now let the group as a whole interact with each other about their questions, opinions, and reactions to having friends of the opposite gender.

GROWING BY DOING 20–25 minutes

Personal Friendships and Boundaries
Explain that one of the things we learn from social science research is that there is a limited number of friends that we can be intimate with, or we spread ourselves too thin. It is interesting that Jesus chose only a few to be in His inner circle when His task to proclaim God to the world was so expansive. Perhaps it indicates how important it is to establish appropriate boundaries with our friends, without becoming too exclusive in the process. Making choices about our own inner circle of friends, keeping appropriate boundaries and setting up helpful guidelines is an important way to be responsible about our current friendships.

Explain that this is a personal exercise for group members to do on their own. If group members need help on this item, refer them to the following example.

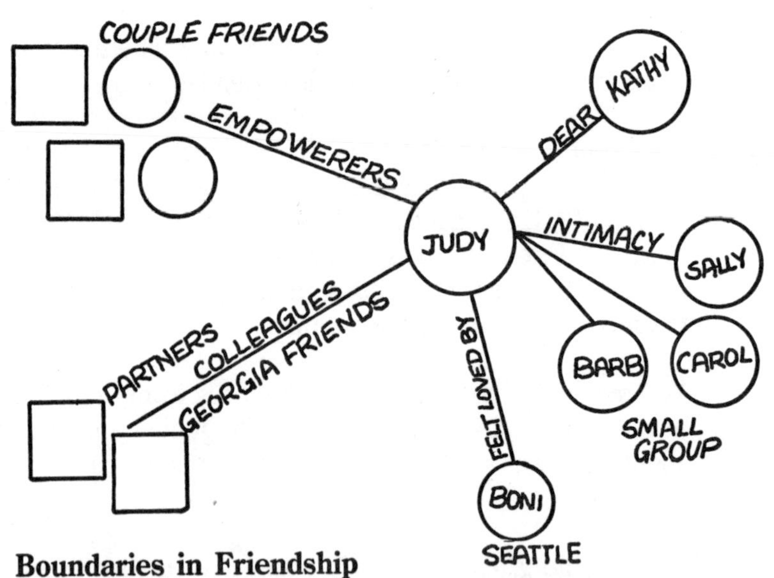

Boundaries in Friendship

This is a time to apply the idea of establishing healthy boundaries with friends as well as to set up appropriate guidelines for same and opposite gender friends. The four major categories of intimacy: intellectual, emotional, physical, and spiritual help students make distinctions between kinds of intimacy between friends. An awareness of some "red flag" areas regarding gender concerns will help group members in their choices about these friendships.

Brainstorm as a group and decide on some basic guidelines for intimacy with same and opposite gender friends. Here are some guidelines to add if the group doesn't address them:

- ❑ No secrets kept about what's happening in the relationship. Be honest with yourself, the other person, and your spouse if you are married.

- ❑ Marriage always has priority for married people. It is important to be aware of the current health of the marriage relationship when engaged in intimate friendships with others.

- ❑ Respect the most strongly felt limits of either friend and don't push that person beyond what his or her boundary is.

- ❑ Be honest with your motives or intention in the friendship and share this with your friend.

- ❑ Can you talk to your important others about what you do in private with your friend?
- ❑ Is the touching comfortable for both parties?
- ❑ Is this relationship one that encourages mutual growth and development?
- ❑ Do you have other friends and mutual friends that you enjoy?

GOING THE SECOND MILE

How to Be a Better Friend
Ask group members to think about a particular friend they would like to talk to about some matter in their friendship.

Optional—Warm Fuzzies
Encourage group members to send a warm fuzzy to a friend. Have postcards or simple paper and envelopes for members to write a special caring message to a special friend they remembered during this exercise.

FOUR

Christian Mothering and Fathering

The redefinition of gender roles has served to challenge overly sharp distinctions between how fathers and mothers are to be involved with their children. A 1990 study for *Christianity Today* found that the vast majority of both female and male respondents "shared equally" in administering discipline (71% and 81% respectively), giving attention to children's spiritual growth and development (72% and 86%), listening to children's problems when they are hurting (65% and 78%), and playing with children (75% and 86%). In each of these areas of parent-child involvement, fathers more than mothers believe that the male contributes an equal share to child care.

It is noteworthy that while there are no parenting tasks reported to be done mainly by husbands, both males and females report that it is mainly the mother who changes diapers, coordinates children's schedules, cares for children (dresses, feeds, bathes), and takes care of other parenting duties.

Do men actually involve themselves more in these parenting activities when the wife works outside the home? In comparing homes, we found that when mothers work outside the home, husbands report helping out more in coordinating children's schedules and caring for them, though wives' reports would dispute that perception. The sharing of the six parenting tasks—administering discipline, listening to problems, playing with the children, changing diapers, giving attention to spiritual development, and managing needs such as clothes shopping—changes little even if the mother works outside the home. In the vast majority of cases, then, women have the same child-rearing responsibilities, whether they work outside the home or not. A 1990 article in *Newsweek* on the "reluctant father" reported similar findings. While 74% of dads surveyed said they "should share child-care chores equally with the mother," only 13% do so.

Since the industrial revolution, most children living in urban areas have been deprived of daytime contact with their fathers. With an increasing number of mothers now working outside the home, the issue of who is to care for children has heightened. In analyzing responses from *Christianity Today* readers we find disagreement over whether working outside the home adversely affects parenting. While an equal number of females agree and disagree with the statement, "Working women with young children are less effective as mothers," males are much more likely to agree (52%) than disagree (31%) with this statement. We also found evidence that an overwhelming majority (nearly 80%) of male and female respondents agree that both fatherhood and motherhood have been devalued in contemporary society.

As **Group Leader** of this small group experience, *you* have a choice as to which elements will best fit your group, your style of leadership, and your purposes. After you examine the **Session Objectives**, select the activities under each heading with which to begin your community building. You have many choices.

SESSION OBJECTIVES

- √ To realize the importance our mother and father had in shaping our own image of who we are as a male or female.
- √ To become aware of how the roles we play as mothers and fathers help to shape our children's masculine or feminine self-concepts.
- √ To gain an understanding of God as parent and how He relates to us as children.
- √ To seek to base our parenting on a biblical model.

GETTING ACQUAINTED 20–30 minutes

Have a group member read aloud **Mothering and Fathering.** Then choose one of the following activities to help create a more comfortable, nonthreatening atmosphere.

When You Were a Child
Ask members of the group to describe the relationship between themselves and their mothers while they were growing up. Next, ask group members to describe their relationship with their fathers as they were growing up. Note patterns of similarities and differences in how persons experience relating to their mothers and fathers.

Ask group members to share the one thing they would most like to have been different in their relationship with their mothers or fathers. Note patterns of similarities and differences in what is expressed.

When You Are a Parent
Ask group members to share the one thing they do best as a parent. Next, ask members to share the one thing they wish they would do better as a parent. Note patterns of similarities and differences, especially between males and females.

GAINING INSIGHT 20–25 minutes

Understanding God As Parent
Explain that an all too common method of presenting a "biblical" model on parenting consists of picking out verses from Scripture and then arranging them as one would arrange flowers. Such "bouquets" of Bible verses are then presented to support the particular point of view held by the arranger. Such methods often do little more than reflect a traditional cultural stereotype which encourages mothers to love and nurture and fathers to take charge of the discipline. How much more fruitful it would be if we would simply use God's model of parenting as our example.

Share that Myron Chartier in his article, "Parenting: A Theological Model" (*Journal of Psychology and Theology,* 1978), has written most informatively by chronicling the biblical evidence in support of the position that God models parenting in seven ways. As you discuss the image of God as parent, share Chartier's seven ways that God models parenting. Note both the masculine and feminine biblical images used for God as parent. Ask the group to construct an image of fathering based upon biblical references to God as parent and the characteristics of Jesus as a man.

- ❑ First, God *cares* for His children. Although this is preeminently demonstrated in the incarnation, death, and resurrection of Christ, numerous biblical passages stress the caring nature of God (Luke 15:11-32; 1 Peter 5:7).

- ❑ Second, God is *responsive* to human needs as can be seen in the Covenant that was established after the flood (Genesis 9:8-17), in the rescuing of Israel from Egypt (Deuteronomy 32), and by freely giving grace and mercy and restoration (John 3:16; Titus 3:3-7).

- ❑ A third way in which God expresses love is in *giving* Christ, the only begotten Son, and the Holy Spirit as comforter (John 3:16).

- ❑ God also loves by showing *respect* for the creation. The challenge is to value and cherish one another as God's creation. It matters to God that people are poor and oppressed since His desire is that people be free and not dominated or possessed.

- ❑ Fifth, God not only created us but *knows* us intimately as the very image of God (John 1:14; Philippians 2:5-8; Hebrews 2:17-18; 4:15). This knowledge penetrates to the core of our existence (Psalm 44:21; John 2:25).

- ❑ A sixth expression of God's love is *forgiveness* (Hebrews 4:15; Luke 19:41-42; John 3:17).

- ❑ Finally, God *disciplines* us as an expression of love (Proverbs 3:11-12; Hebrews 12:5-8; Revelation 3:19). The discipline of God over Israel can be seen as an attempt to develop a faithful and obedient people.

Explain that God serves as a model to Christian parents, both mothers and fathers. Those who would assign certain of the parenting tasks described above to mothers and others to fathers will not find support for their position in the Bible. Taken as a whole, the biblical emphasis is clearly placed upon the love and grace which God so freely gives. However, this is not a watered-down type of easy love which is void of expectations and demands. God's love includes disciplinary action, action which is meant for the good of the one being disciplined. The action of God as parent clearly points to a model in which parental love and discipline intertwine in encouraging a developing maturity in children. Love and discipline must be shown by both mothers and fathers. If anything, the biblical model of fatherhood points to the necessity of *fathers* assuming a key role in the development of children.

GROWING BY DOING 15–20 minutes

Parenting Tasks

People are different and have different interests and strengths. This difference will also express itself in the way persons enter into their parenting tasks. The purpose of this part of the study is to further develop self-awareness of how each group member's parenting style is a reflection of his or her gender role and how each member might be willing to change.

Have each member of the group share how comfortable they feel with the way in which they responded to each of the eight parenting task statements. Have members identify those tasks which they do best and those which they have the most trouble doing. Have the group discuss ways in which their children either benefited or were deprived due to the way parenting tasks were shared.

GOING THE SECOND MILE 5 minutes

Sentence Completion

Encourage each married couple to spend some time during the next week sharing the ways in which they completed the two sentences in the **Growing By Doing** section. Ask them to attempt to reach agreement about how they desire to share parenting tasks.

Encourage single parents to think on how their close friends might be more meaningfully involved in the lives of their children.

GROWING AS A LEADER

Leadership Assessment

There are two types of leadership tasks which are needed in a small group—instrumental and expressive. *Instrumental leadership tasks* have to do with organizing, pace setting, asking questions, giving direction, summarizing, and maintaining the type of group interaction which will allow it to accomplish its goals.

Expressive or socio-emotional leadership tasks have to do with maintaining good social relationships between group members. Expressive leadership involves affirming and encouraging individuals and resolving any conflict or differences which might arise between members in the group. Research on the family and other small groups show that while males are generally more skilled at instrumental tasks, females are better at performing expressive leadership tasks.

Assess your own instrumental and expressive leadership skills. Is there any evidence of a greater need for either of these tasks in the group? How do other members of the group share in providing needed instrumental or expressive leadership skills? How can you be a more effective instrumental or expressive leader? How can you encourage the development of these skills in other group members?

FIVE

Sexuality and Gender

Sexuality is one way of understanding who we are as male and female. We express our authentic humanness as sexual persons in emotional, physical, and spiritual ways. There is no area of life that concerns us so deeply as our sexuality. We know that even the most meaningful sexual relationship can sometimes seem wrong. Sexuality brings out such divergent expressions as joy and guilt, self-esteem and self-rejection, exuberance and repression.

This forbidden topic of sex has been brought out of the privacy of the bedrooms into the public arena, giving us an opportunity in this small group session to ask important questions about what it means to be created male and female sexual beings.

Decisions about sexual expression are often the source of anxiety and controversy. All members of our small group struggle with how to be authentic sexual people. We live in a secular environment that influences our sexual value system. Messages received from family, friends, church, and society can lead to unhealthy attitudes about sexuality. We need to base our values, beliefs, and behaviors on sound information and biblical principles. Satisfaction comes as we live out these values in a consistent person-centered way.

As **Group Leader** of this small group experience, *you* have a choice as to which elements will best fit your group, your style of leadership, and your purposes. After you examine the **Session Objectives**, select the activities under each heading with which to begin your community building. You have many choices.

SESSION OBJECTIVES

- √ To identify messages from various sources that determine our sexual attitudes and beliefs.
- √ To consider gender differences in messages received about body image and sexuality.
- √ To reflect on biblical passages that refer to body image and sexual expression and glean new understanding.
- √ To affirm and appreciate the opposite gender through gaining insight into their experiences of sexual development.
- √ To promote decision-making that is person-centered and biblically-based.

GETTING ACQUAINTED 20–30 minutes

Have a group member read aloud **Created As Sexual Beings.** Then choose one of the following activities to help create a more comfortable, nonthreatening atmosphere.

Pocket Principle

1 **There is a close relationship between how people feel about their bodies and their self-esteem. Positive feelings about one's self and one's body will determine a person's capacity for sexual and emotional intimacy. Healthy sexuality requires a positive integration of body and self-image. Accepting our sexual selves and making value based decisions about sexual expression leads to a confident and positive self-esteem.**

Messages About Sexuality

This first exercise helps group members recognize the various messages they have received from church, home, friends, and society at large. When nothing is said about sex in the home or at church, it is probably a message indicating that sex is a taboo topic and not seen as an integral part of God's good creation. It is also important to be aware of gender differences in these messages. For example, the double standard suggests that some behavior is all right for males but not for females. Other messages put the responsibility for setting limits on the female rather than the joint responsibility of both genders.

Affirmation of Body Self-Image

Body image and sexuality may still be a difficult topic for some group members to talk about, so special time for personal reflection is incorporated in this session. This section on body image is a way of helping individuals reflect on messages they personally received about their bodies. This has a significant impact on the ability to accept oneself and one's sexuality.

In same gender groups, focus on how personal affirmation and/or depreciation of our bodies impacts our sexual development, attitudes, and feelings about our sexual selves.

In mixed gender groups, share and compare the kinds of messages that were given to males and females about their bodies. Ask: **Are there some typical gender stereotypes?**

Optional—Describe Your Body

If your group has not developed to a point of cohesion or comfort, you may try a less threatening exercise. Have members describe their bodies in terms of the following opposites:

- ❑ soft or hard
- ❑ warm or cold
- ❑ young or old
- ❑ active or passive
- ❑ strong or weak
- ❑ penetrable or defended
- ❑ positive or negative
- ❑ public or private
- ❑ touchable or untouchable

Now have group members discuss what they learned about themselves as they reflect on their summary descriptions.

Optional—Body Parts
This exercise is perhaps even more explicit than **Affirmation of Body Self-Image.** It may be appropriate if you have a group that wants to go deeper with this body image focus.

Ask group members to imagine looking at themselves in a mirror. Have them consider their various body parts from head to toe and indicate whether they have positive or negative feelings about each part.

Next, have them list anonymously on a piece of paper the three body parts they are least satisfied with and three body parts they are most satisfied with. A designated recorder will tally the responses and report the findings to the entire group under the categories Less Liked and More Liked.

Now, bring the group together to discuss the findings. In general, did members find it easier to come up with negative or positive reactions to body parts? Were there particular concerns about their sexual parts? Do you think males or females were more negative or positive about their bodies? Is the group surprised by any of the results? Do you agree with the statement, "How you feel about your body determines how you feel about yourself!" Why or why not?

Be alert to the member who does not wish to share and be careful that you do not ask any questions that would put him or her on the spot. Statistics indicate that one out of seven men and one out of four women have experienced some kind of sexual abuse. This means it is very likely that someone in your group has been abused. Make a sensitive statement recognizing the fact that sexual abuse is a very painful and intrusive experience. Be available at the end of the session in case anyone would like to remain after the group has been dismissed to share any discomfort about this session.

GAINING INSIGHT 20–25 minutes

Scripture Study
This section focuses on biblical passages that will help group members see how sexuality is dealt with in an open and affirming way (Song of Songs and Genesis). Sexuality is part of the whole person! Gender equality is an important aspect of marital sexuality as seen in 1 Corinthians 7:3-5.

Normative Principles for Sexual Expression
The three normative principles of Smedes are used to reiterate these relational themes and give the group a chance to discuss how these values become important when making decisions about sexual expressions. Mary Stewart Van Leeuwen (*Radix,* Nov/Dec 1984, vol. 16, no. 3, p. 11) relates these normative patterns with responsible decision-making. She rephrases these principles as follows:

- ❑ The sexuality of every person is meant to be woven into the whole character of that person and integrated into his/her quest for human values.

- ❑ The sexuality of every person is meant to be an urge toward and a means of expressing a deep personal relationship with another person.

- ❑ The sexuality of every person is meant to move him/her toward a heterosexual union of committed (permanent) love.

Explain that our society has depersonalized and dehumanized sexuality and we need to make decisions that will enhance the personhood of others in their relationships. Making decisions about sexual behavior and expression needs to be carefully thought through so we can live consistently as God intended.

Making Decisions About Sexual Expression
Van Leeuwen suggests that "when physical sex is severed from the rest of a person's life . . . when it is shoved into a compartment of its own, isolated from a living bond with other needs and goals, sexuality is an abnormal experience" (p. 11). Therefore, these biblical (normal) patterns lead to

authentic sexual expression and give guidelines for individual and responsible decision-making.

Now, ask the group members to brainstorm together and list specific guidelines that will help them make responsible person-centered decisions about sexual expression. Supplement their list with the following suggested guidelines.

- ❑ Ability to choose freely. Make personal choices rather than relying on or being forced by others.
- ❑ Ability to consider all the alternatives and different ways of looking at issues.
- ❑ Ability to consider the consequences of each alternative, such as public censure, loss of relationship, physical danger.
- ❑ Ability to make a choice that makes you feel good about the other, yourself, and the relationship.
- ❑ Ability to make a decision and follow through with consistent behavior.
- ❑ Ability to share your choices with others and live comfortably with biblical principles.

GROWING BY DOING (20-25 minutes)

Growing Up the Opposite Gender

This exercise gives group members a chance to consider what it might have been like to grow up the opposite gender, especially in regard to sexuality. You will need to get the group sufficiently relaxed so they will be able to image this experience. So, take your time. Talk slowly in a comfortable voice and say:

- ❑ **Get yourself in a relaxed position. Place your feet flat on floor, hands relaxed in lap, and eyes closed. Take some deep breaths and give yourself permission to relax and let yourself be open to this experience.**

- ❑ Remember the rhyme, "What are little boys made of? What are little girls made of?" Well, let's imagine that you are born the opposite gender of who you now are. What would life be like for you as this gender? How would things have been different for you?

- ❑ Imagine your mother being pregnant with you. What are her thoughts and hopes about your gender? Does your father want a boy or girl? What are their thoughts, attitudes, and feelings about the gender of this new baby?

- ❑ Now you are actually being delivered and the announcement is made—"Congratulations! You have a new baby girl!" or "You have a new baby boy!" How do your parents respond to this announcement? How do other important family members respond? Does it matter that you are this gender for any particular reasons? Do grandparents or siblings have an investment in what your gender is? What is your body like as a male/female?

- ❑ Now you are growing up. You are acquainted with yourself and your body. How do you express yourself as male/female? Are you treated in special ways due to your gender? Are there special games, activities, interests, and things you do because of your gender? How do you like your body? Are you allowed to go nude around the house? What are the attitudes in the family about sexuality? Does it affect you in a special way because of your gender? Are there certain comments made to you about your body specific to your gender?

- ❑ Now you are growing older and school is important to you. How do your teachers and peers respond to you as this gender? What kind of games do you play and with whom?

- ❑ Now you have reached puberty. What are the physical changes going on in your body and how do you feel about them? What do others tell you about your

sexuality, about self-stimulation? How do you feel in this new body? How is your life different now that you have become more obviously sexually mature? Who talks to you about sexual matters? Where do you learn about sexual expression?

- ❑ **What does your new sexual development mean as far as relationships with the opposite sex? In regard to dating? How do you become close and intimate with your friends? What are your thoughts about future career, marriage, or single life? What are your thoughts about having children?**

- ❑ **Now, it's time to end this exercise and change back again to your real gender and your real body. You will have a chance to share anything you would like about going through this imagery. I will start counting backward from 5 to 1. When I get to 1 you will become your original gender once again. 5 . . . 4 . . . 3 . . . 2 . . . 1! Open your eyes and you are your own self once again.**

Have members get with one other person to share anything they wish about this experience.

Reassemble the group and ask: **What were the positive and negative feelings you had about being the opposite gender?** Help the group process their new insight and understanding about the opposite gender. Many will express difficulty in imagining sexual differences. Some men may feel the loss of not being able to bear children; some women may feel they would have much more power and freedom as a male. Help group members appreciate the gender differences and gain better understanding of what it means to grow up male/female in our culture.

GOING THE SECOND MILE 5 minutes

Living As a Sexual Person
Remind group members to apply the things learned during this session to their personal lives. Encourage them to list specific guidelines that will help them in their own decision-making process about their sexual expression.

SIX

Where Is the Spouse I Thought I Married?

What has traditionally been defined as male and female rights and duties in marriage can no longer be assumed. In response, some married couples are tempted to retreat out of fear to a traditional patriarchal form of marriage in which gender roles are sharply separated. While it may be tempting to return to a time that appears to have been less disruptive, this course of action offers a false sense of comfort, for women especially have had a very difficult life in the past. Christians need to see the present disruption as an opportunity to put in place a more biblically based form of marriage life.

A 1990 *Christianity Today* research study, based upon responses from its subscribers, points to the areas of conflict in contemporary marriage. When asked to identify the issues of greatest concern, a large majority expressed concern about working women who were mothers of young children. With trends showing a steady rise in the number of wives working outside the home, it is hardly surprising that dividing household duties between working spouses also emerged as a key issue for respondents. Over 90% of both male and female respondents agreed with the statement, "When both husband and wife work full-time they should share equally in parenting and household tasks." In principle then, those surveyed believe that husbands and wives should equally shoulder parenting and household tasks when both work.

However, when this view is compared with the respondents' answers to specific statements about actual practice, only moderate shifting of household responsibility is found to occur when the wife works full-time. Females and males report that when the wife works, husbands do participate more in household tasks such as vacuuming, washing dishes, and cooking meals. A majority of male and female respondents, not surprisingly, identify doing the yard work and maintaining the car as mainly the husband's responsibilities. It is significant, however, that men and women differ in the amount of household work they do even when the wife works. This is consistent with a recent study that found that husbands of working wives spend an average of only 20 minutes more per day working in the home than husbands of nonworking wives.

Since parenting and housework entails considerably more than 40 minutes per day, working wives frequently do double duty. In her book, *The Second Shift* (Viking Press, 1989) based on a study of middle-class couples, Arlie Hochschild concluded that instead of having it all, most working wives are merely *doing* it all.

As **Group Leader** of this small group experience, *you* have a choice as to which elements will best fit your group, your style of leadership, and your purposes. After you examine the **Session Objectives,** select the activities under each heading with which to begin your community building. You have many choices.

SESSION OBJECTIVES

- √ To respect the way in which God has created each person as a unique individual.
- √ To further realize that there is no definitive marriage relationship.
- √ To compare the expectations of traditional marriages with the expectations of marriages defined by modern secular thought.
- √ To search for biblical principles for how women and men are to be within marriage.
- √ To want to become and to allow one's spouse to become the person God created her or him to be.

GETTING ACQUAINTED 20–30 minutes

Have a group member read aloud **Supermen and Superwomen.** Then choose one of the following activities to help create a more comfortable, nonthreatening atmosphere.

Do Opposites Attract?
Explain that some couples know very well how they are alike and how they are different from each other. Others, however, have a tendency to see their spouses in gender role stereotypes. Giving group members a chance to list the ways in which they are both alike and different from their spouses will help them get in touch with the real spouse they married.

After everyone has had a chance to complete their lists, ask each to note examples of where similarities or differences are contrary to traditional gender role stereotypes. For instance, if "competitiveness" was listed as a way in which a couple were alike, this would be against the gender role cultural stereotype which calls for women to be noncompetitive. Another example would be a marriage in which the husband verbally expressed affection more than the wife.

If time permits, ask group members to share the ways in which they perceive their marriage relationships to be based on traditional or nontraditional gender role ideals. It will be both fun and fascinating to allow spouses to indicate to the group where they agree or disagree in their perception of the ways they are alike or different from each other.

GAINING INSIGHT 20–25 minutes

Traditional Vs. Modern Marital Roles
The purpose of this section of study is to encourage group members to examine their views of marital roles in light of a biblical view of marriage and relationships.

A Christian Alternative
Have group members fill in the middle column of the chart with a word or brief description of what they consider an alternative biblical ideal marriage to be. An example of brief descriptions which might be given are shown in the following chart.

CHARACTERISTICS OF TRADITIONAL, BIBLICAL IDEAL, AND MODERN MARRIAGES

TRADITIONAL	BIBLICAL IDEAL	MODERN
	Marital Commitment	
Commitment to marriage as an institution	COVENANT (Between) Partners)	Contract (Self-fulfillment)
Coercive	Cohesive	Disengaged
Dutiful Sex (Male Pleasure)	Affectionate Sex (Mutual Pleasure)	Self-Centered Sex (Personal Pleasure)
	Marital Roles and Adaptability	
Law	GRACE	Anarchy
Predetermined (Role Segregation)	Creative (Interchangeable Roles)	Undetermined (Undifferentiated Roles)
Rigid/Stilted	Adaptable/Flexible	Chaotic
	Marital Authority	
Ascribed Power	EMPOWERING	Possessive Power
Authoritarian Male Headship	Mutual Submissiveness (interdependence)	No Authority (neither submissive)
Male Centered	Relationship Centered	Self-Centered

Marital Communication

Inexpressiveness	INTIMACY	Pseudo-Intimacy
Pronouncement (Legislate)	Discussion (Negotiate)	Declaration (Stalemate)
Nonassertive	Assertive	Aggressive

Marital Commitment

After group members have completed their descriptions, discuss each of the characteristics, supplementing with the following information.

Marital Commitment The key word which expresses the biblical basis for marital commitment is *covenant.* God intends for married persons to not merely be committed to the institution of marriage, but to make an unconditional commitment to each other. Marriage is not based upon a contract, which is a conditional commitment. In a marriage based upon contract, the two persons agree to stay in the marriage only so long as the other person fulfills his or her end of the bargain or as long as the marriage proves to meet his or her needs.

A marriage based on a covenant commitment will not be held together by coercive force, nor will it be disengaged due to each partner's selfish preoccupation with self-fulfillment. In a marriage based on a covenant commitment, two people will be *cohesive*—bonded together on the security that each has committed his and her life to the other. With an emphasis on mutual pleasure, affectionate sex will characterize a biblical marriage, as opposed to dutiful sex and male pleasure in the traditional marriage, and self-centered sex and personal pleasure in the modern marriage.

Marital Roles and Adaptability In traditional marriage, the roles are usually segregated, with the husband assuming the role of working outside the home, and the wife assuming the role of homemaking and caring for the children. Marital roles in the modern marriage are undifferentiated—there is no agreement designating which marriage partner will assume a given responsibility. Responsibility is often worked out within a system of social exchanges—"I'll do the dishes tonight if you will iron the clothes." The traditional marriage can be described in terms of law and rigidity, the modern marriage by anarchy and chaos.

Assigning tasks on the basis of a person's interests, skills, or availability is a loving way to work out marital roles. It also respects differences and recognizes the unique talents which God has given each spouse to contribute in special ways to the marital relationship.

Marital Authority Authority in marriage is currently a controversial issue among Christians. The basis of authority is *power,* the ability to influence another person. Power is conventionally used to control another person. The biblical model for the use of power is *empowering*—to build another person up.

Authority in Christian marriage involves dual submission to the lordship of Jesus Christ and to one another. From Ephesians 5, it is clear that headship, if that is the view one espouses, is to be understood not in the hierarchical sense of the husband's lording it over his wife, but rather in the sense of taking the role of a suffering servant. Christ's example as a compassionate servant who gave His life for His bride, the church, is the same self-giving, suffering-servant role. Mutual submissiveness then, is the overriding message of Ephesians 5.

Marital Communication In a balanced marriage, the partners will communicate by expressing themselves in a caring and concerned manner. When one talks, the other will listen. They will want what is best for their partner. Differences will be dealt with by respecting the other's needs and desires. There will be an effort to understand each other's point of view and to respond with empathy.

The capacity for marriage partners to communicate feelings freely and openly with each other is contingent upon trust and commitment. Then they are not afraid to share and be intimate with one another. This brings us back to the unconditional covenant love which is the cornerstone for marital communication and honest sharing without the threat of rejection. As partners offer their love unconditionally to each other, the security that is established will lead to deeper levels of intimacy.

GROWING BY DOING 15–20 minutes

Complete the Statement
Have all men in the group sit in a circle to share and discuss their responses to what they find most and least inviting in the traditional and modern marriage. Ask the women in the group to sit outside the circle and merely observe. Next, have all the women in the group sit in a circle to share and discuss their responses to what they find most and least inviting in the traditional and modern marriage. Ask the men to sit outside of the circle and merely observe.

Then give both women and men a chance to share their observations of watching members of the opposite gender interact. Note gender differences in the interaction which was observed.

GOING THE SECOND MILE 5 minutes

Talking Ideals
Encourage each married couple to spend some time during the next few days thinking about ways in which they can better fulfill God's ideal for them in their marriage. Suggest to couples that they might covenant together regarding the ways in which they can best be who God wants them to be for each other. Encourage group members to pray for each other during the week. Encourage single persons to take an inventory of the supportive trusting relationships they have in their lives.

GROWING AS A LEADER

Growth Evaluation
It has been suggested that the biblical themes of covenant, grace, empowering, and intimacy can be used to understand

what a man and a woman are to be to each other in a Christian marriage. These same themes can be useful in evaluating the maturity of relationships within a small group. Healthy small groups are those within which:

❑ Relationships are growing toward *covenant*—unconditional mutual commitments.

❑ Relationships are maintained within an atmosphere of *grace* which embraces acceptance and forgiveness.

❑ The resources of group members are used to *empower* rather than to control other members.

❑ There is an *intimacy* which leads to knowing, caring, understanding, communication, and communion with other members of the group.

Evaluate the growth which the group has made thus far. Evaluate your relationship with group members on the basis of each of these four themes. How do you express your sense of commitment to the group? Do group members experience a sense of acceptance and forgiveness from you? Do they experience you as an empowering leader? Would they characterize you as a person who knows, cares, and understands them?

As you reflect upon yourself as a leader, ask God to enable you to develop a leadership style which is characterized by covenant commitment, grace, empowering, and intimacy.

SEVEN

My Boss Is a Woman! My Boss Is a Man!

One of the issues of importance in any study of gender is the effect of gender on work relationships. In this session, we will focus on various effects, attempting to stimulate observation and recognition of stereotypes, as well as exploring the scriptural basis for a different way of viewing work and people.

Does God think that any particular kind of work is better than other kinds? Do we? In our Western culture, we often tend to see intellectual work as better than manual labor, but this may be a form of cultural or social snobbery rather than a helpful standard for the true value of work. Also, paid work is sometimes viewed as better than unpaid work. Is this a Christian view of work, or have we incorporated this faulty view of the value of work from our culture?

God made humankind, male and female, and placed them in the Garden. Their work, subduing and having dominion (Genesis 1:28), was both manual (taking care of the animals and plants) and intellectual (naming the animals). It is pretty clear that Adam and Eve were to share the work, and no mention is made of a salary for doing any of these tasks! Scripture also makes it clear in many places that workers are to be paid what they are worth. Jesus, in sending out the disciples, told them to eat what the householders served them, because laborers deserved to be paid (Luke 10:7).

Have we maligned some forms of work? Are women often relegated to menial tasks? Do men stereotypically end up in the overseer positions, possibly domineering over women and also other men? How can we as Christians reframe our view of work, so that it includes a balanced view of servanthood, while not making doormats or slavemasters out of any of us?

As **Group Leader** of this small group experience, *you* have a choice as to which elements will best fit your group, your style of leadership, and your purposes. After you examine the **Session Objectives**, select the activities under each heading with which to begin your community building. You have many choices.

SESSION OBJECTIVES

- √ To introduce and explore scriptural models of work.
- √ To share experiences that help us understand in what ways gender may influence work in our society.
- √ To potentially begin reframing our valuations of work.

GETTING ACQUAINTED 20–30 minutes

Have a group member read aloud **Gender in the Workplace.** Then choose one of the following activities to help create a more comfortable, nonthreatening atmosphere.

Who's the Boss?
Pair group members up with people they're comfortable with, yet haven't spent much time with. Ask the pairs to talk about someone for whom they are working or have worked for in the past. Encourage them to discuss the questions.

Optional—Fears in a Hat
This is a game with an intrinsic way to reduce the anxiety level and raise the level of willingness to share deeper things.

Have each group member write a fear related to a work relationship on a slip of paper and put it in a hat (or similar anonymous-making container!). Pull out the slips and read the fears. Discuss the following questions.

- ❑ **Are there any similarities or differences in fears?**
- ❑ **Is there an obvious grouping of fears?**
- ❑ **Are there any distinctly female or male fears?**

GAINING INSIGHT

Scripture Study
Have the group read Proverbs 31:10-31. Point out that the housewife is extolled for buying property, producing goods, being an effective business manager, organizing the sundry activities of an entire household, and being reliable in maintenance tasks. She is a philanthropist, which means she has excess available for distribution. Help the group members see that this passage can be read either traditionally or nontraditionally depending on the inclination of the reader, not necessarily based on the passage itself.

Then read 1 Timothy 3:1-13. Consider reversing the gender of the passage and reading it to the group to determine how it feels.

GROWING BY DOING

What Is Work?
Ask group members to share their insights on the questions in this section. This should provide for some lively discussion.

Finish the Story
Reproduce the following stories on separate sheets and distribute John's Story to half the group and Joan's Story to the other half. Keep it a secret that there are two versions. After group members have completed the stories, have them compare their endings. Discuss any differences. Note that typically, stories finished with a male protagonist are ended much more happily than female protagonists:

John's Story

John is a medical student at a premier medical school. He is dating another medical student who is in the same class. Every year, the school puts out a list of the top 10 students in the class, and this year John discovers that the person he is dating is #2 and John himself is #1 in the class. John . . .

Joan's Story

Joan is a medical student at a premier medical school. She is dating another medical student who is in the same class. Every year, the school puts out a list of the top 10 students in the class, and this year Joan discovers that the person she is dating is #2 and Joan herself is #1 in the class. Joan . . .

Optional—Work Constellation Exercise

Suzette Haden Elgin in *The Gentle Art of Verbal Self Defense* (Dorset, 1980) has an entire chapter on making a constellation map of your employment situation. Simply have group members put their names at the center of a page, and then identify an organizational structure to whom they are responsible, officially or unofficially. Discuss these questions.

- ❑ **In whose graces do you need to stay?**
- ❑ **Who is not your boss but can tell you to do something?**
- ❑ **How do others organize your time for you?**
- ❑ **How many men and women must you take into account to make decisions?**

GOING THE SECOND MILE

Writing Assignment

Remind group members to write a psalm or a devotional prayer of no more than 50 words for the next session. If you have a group of mixed gender, each person should write as if he or she were the opposite gender. If your group is all one gender, some of the group will write as if they were the opposite gender, some as their own gender.

Worship Symbol

Also remind group members to bring some sort of worship symbol or object which represents their investment in this group.

Work Smarter
Encourage group members to "work smarter" during the coming weeks by being more aware of how gender affects their work relationships.

GROWING AS A LEADER

Personal Assessment
Your role as **Group Leader** will be important as you close. How are *you* feeling about the group?

In what ways has it been a growing experience for you? For the rest of the group?

What kinds of joyful experiences have you and your group had?

You will need to think through these issues in order to tie up loose ends and plan a future as a "former" group.

EIGHT

Gender and Spiritual Maturity

Western culture tends to think of persons as either completely materialistic, or as immortal souls temporarily trapped in bodies. They either deny the spirit, or they deny the body. Christianity affirms the body as good and as genuinely being *us* and not a sort of prison, while condemning the *flesh* or carnal nature.

Some people think of spirituality as the denial of the body, rather than the denial of the selfish carnal nature. Certain good ascetic practices (like fasting, silence, etc.) can be easily misunderstood as being a form of hatred of the physical, rather than a healthy discipline of the body and mind. Likewise, virginity and celibacy can become the desexualization of the spiritual person; these practices are intended as a focusing (1 Corinthians 7:32-34).

Some denominations (Greek Orthodox and Episcopal, for example) have less struggle with this physical aspect of the spiritual life due to their greater sense of persons being fully spiritual. This belief in humanity's being both an embodied soul and ensouled body manifests itself in a greater vivaciousness and sensuality inherent in the spiritual life. Having a physical worship symbol or object for the closing session is an attempt to combine these two elements.

More than this, however, Session 8 is designed to overcome certain stereotyped messages given to women and men which are hindrances to spiritual maturity. One of the alternate activities is designed to give members a richer understanding of God by multiplying metaphors. This will hopefully allow us to recognize the diversity of our experiences of God and rethink the messages which we received "with our mother's milk" as we grew up.

Nowhere is it taught in Scripture that we are to become "doormats for Jesus"; likewise, we are not commanded to be "Lone Rangers for God." Relationships are not "at any price," and our God-given dominion must not become a demonic domination. If humanity is intrinsically social (and Genesis 1:26-27 teaches us that this is so), then either of these extremes dehumanize us, and only a person who is whole can be holy.

As **Group Leader** of this small group experience, *you* have a choice as to which elements will best fit your group, your style of leadership, and your purposes. After you examine the **Session Objectives**, select the activities under each heading with which to begin your community building. You have many choices.

SESSION OBJECTIVES

- √ To become aware of the rich diversity of metaphors for God which are available to enhance our spiritual devotion.
- √ To recognize hindrances to holiness and patterns of sin which are culturally exacerbated.
- √ To define spirituality as something which permeates all of life, and includes us as physical and sexual persons.
- √ To provide an opportunity for members to express themselves to God and to each other in appreciation for both their gender and the group.

GETTING ACQUAINTED 20–30 minutes

This is your last group meeting, and if your group has developed genuine trust and friendships, you will want to emphasize moving together more personally and connecting face-to-face about more genuinely probing issues. In light of this, have a group member read aloud **Barriers to Holiness.** Then pick an appropriate activity from the following.

Two areas are covered in this section: hindrances to holiness and images of God. If you were to ask the group to name some things which are marks of maturity or which hinder holiness, you would get a wide range of answers. Hopefully, this session will allow some consensus to come forth.

Common Definitions

Ask group members to get with at least one other person and tell him or her about their most spiritual experience. Have the pairs consider any similarities between their answers. Did they define spirituality in the same way?

Point out that when we have an idea of how other people think about God, we have enriched our own understanding of who God is. This should increase our devotion to God; it should make us more spiritual.

Optional—God Is an Electric Can Opener

If your group has not connected well during the eight sessions, this is a nonthreatening alternative. First, take a moment to define the word *metaphor*. Explain that a metaphor is a way of describing something by saying that it is something else. For example, Jesus is the door. Since we all know that Jesus isn't actually a door, we recognize the meaning that this metaphor conveys. Now, display the following items for the group to see.

flower	book	beverage	food
building	animal	ice cream	vehicle
sport	clock	game	home appliance
coin	clothing	light source	song
art form	road	musical instrument	newspaper section

Have each person tell the group how the item is a metaphor for God, which sort of item God would be if He were that item, and why. For example, if God were a window, He might be a big bay window to see everything, or a tiny window bringing sunlight into a jail cell, or a storefront window inviting people to come inside. Of course, there are no wrong answers in this. If a group member is stumped, have the whole group brainstorm.

GAINING INSIGHT 20–25 minutes

Models of Spirituality

Have group members read the Scripture passages and identify what the listed persons are doing which shows spiritual maturity. In each case, the passage cited is an affirmation of the accurate discernment and spiritual insight of the person, although one might also note their willingness to obey God.

Now have the group members add their own choices to the list. Ask each person to name a person he or she considers to be spiritual, and say why they think so. Ask: **Are there any gender differences in a description of these persons?**

Now have group members read Genesis 3:16-19. Encourage them to write down any ideas they might have about male sin as compared to female sin. Referring back to their listing of other spiritually mature people, ask: **Why did you choose a male or female?** Then discuss the questions on male and female spirituality.

Point out that a common understanding of the description of the Fall (which is not a prescription of how God wants it to be) is that the typically female sin will be dependence, self-negation, and over-connectedness, while the typically male sin will be pride, detachment, and workaholism. *Gender and Grace* (Mary Stewart Van Leeuwen, IVP, 1990) is a very helpful book on this topic. Ask: **Since it was only in recent medical history that women were allowed anesthesia during labor, how do we understand the work of Christ as overcoming the results of the Fall?**

As your group works through the two charts in this section, try to determine whether everyone is operating out of the same model! Your group members may not all be operating with the same understanding when it comes to spiritual maturity! Be aware of this while leading the discussion. The Target model is more biblically accurate, and is closer to the New Testament word for *sin* which means "to miss the mark," but many people think in terms of the Polar model.

GROWING BY DOING

Celebrate Your Gender
Collect all the writing assignments from last session and mix them up so that no one can tell whose poem or prayer is being read. Have group members try to tell if the psalm was written from the perspective of a woman or a man.

Next, have each member share his or her worship object or symbol. This should not be rushed. After all have shared their gifts, close with prayer.

GOING THE SECOND MILE

Empowered by Prayer
Have group members choose another person in the group and make a commitment to pray regularly for him or her.

GROWING AS A LEADER

Some people will not want the study to end. Others will feel they have committed all the time needed for this subject. If your group wishes to continue on this topic, share some other resources, or look for other titles in the GroupBuilder series which are of interest to your group, and help them find a time to organize a follow-up group.